Preliminary Hearings in Pennsylvania: A Handbook for Defense Counsel

2009 Edition

By
T. AXEL JONES, ESQ.

Member of the Pennsylvania Bar

Paul Revere Publishing
Pennsylvania

ABOUT THE AUTHOR

T. Axel Jones, Esq. received his B.A. in Philosophy from Mansfield University and his Juris Doctorate from the Dickinson School of Law of the Pennsylvania State University. He is admitted to the Bar of the Supreme Court of Pennsylvania.

Axel is the editor of the Third Edition of Pennsylvania Drunk Driving, a PA DUI Manual by Attorney Patrick F. Lauer. He is currently employed as counsel in the Law Offices of Fisher & Fisher in Monroe County, Pennsylvania.

THANKS

Pat, Marlin and Josh.
Marshall, Nick, Bill and Mary.
Tim I & Tim II, Shelli, Katie, Cindy, Donna, Elaine, and Paula.
Erik, Gillian, and Anita.

FOREWORD

This book is intended for Defense Counsel of all levels of experience and training preparing for a Preliminary Hearing. While this book is generally applicable for Hearings anywhere in the Commonwealth of Pennsylvania, the local rules and procedures should always be consulted. Philadelphia District Justice and municipal Courts have their own procedural rules which may not be the same as other jurisdictions. Avoid these local rules at your peril.

This book was created to provide you with accurate and authoritative information concerning the subject matter covered; however, this publication is not a substitute for the advice of qualified defense counsel. If you are in need of competent legal services you should contact a local attorney in your jurisdiction at once. Most local bar associations provide low-cost referrals to experts in your area of need.

Any reference to the "rules" or "Rule" is to the Pennsylvania Rules of Criminal Procedure unless otherwise noted.

References throughout to "District Justice", "Justice", "Authority" or "Issuing Authority" are to the Pennsylvania Magisterial District Justices unless otherwise noted.

T. Axel Jones, Esq.

CITE THIS WORK

Jones,   Preliminary   Hearings   in   PA,   §   _____.

TABLE OF CASES

TABLE OF CASES

TABLE OF CASES

TABLE OF CASES

TABLE OF CASES

TABLE OF CONTENTS

CHAPTER 1
Introduction

CHAPTER 2
Legal Basis for the Preliminary Hearing

CHAPTER 3
Defendant's Rights and Responsibilities

CHAPTER 4
Legal issues at the Preliminary Hearing

CHAPTER 5
Cross-Examination

CHAPTER 6
Presentation of the Defendant's Case

CHAPTER 7
Outcome of the Preliminary Hearing

CHAPTER 7
Post-Preliminary Hearing and Conclusion

1

INTRODUCTION

"The Right to a preliminary examination, though widely recognized in the United States and all English-speaking countries, is not a constitutional right, but rather a right granted by statute."[1]

§ 1-1 Purpose

The primary reason for a preliminary hearing is to protect a person's right against unlawful arrest and detention.[2] Pennsylvania does not want clearly innocent people, or those with no connection to a criminal act to have to endure the expense, time, and frustration of experiencing the criminal justice process. The preliminary hearing then, is a check on the system to prevent such occurrences.[3]   It is not a trial in any sense of the word. It does not purport or attempt to determine the guilt or innocence of the accused, nor is he required to speak, plead or offer testimony in defense.[4]

It is an essential and important part of the Criminal Defendant's processing through the criminal justice system. It is often the first time he or she has access to the formal charges against him or her. It is sometimes the first time a Defendant will speak with an attorney.

---

[1] Orfield, Lester Bernhardt. Criminal Procedure from Arrest to Appeal. NY, NY University Press, 1947, Page 50.

[2] *Commonwealth v. Mullen. 460 Pa. 336 (1975).*

[3] The preliminary hearing seeks to prevent a person from being imprisoned or required to enter bail for a crime which was never committed, or for a crime with which there is no evidence of the person's connection. *Commonwealth ex rel. Maisenholder v. Rundle. 414 Pa. 11, 198 A.2d 134(1981).*

[4] *Commonwealth ex rel. Maisenhelder v. Rundle, 414 Pa. 11, 15, 198 A.2d 565, 567 (1964); Commonwealth v. Rashed, 496 Pa. 26, 32, 436 A.2d 134, 137 (1981).*

INTRODUCTION

"It is axiomatic that the preliminary hearing is a 'critical stage' of a criminal proceeding, at which Appellant is entitled to the assistance of effective counsel."[5]

The Preliminary Hearing is an integral part of every criminal defendant's due process rights.[6] However, absent prejudice from a lack of representation at the preliminary Hearing, the Defendant is entitled to no remedy[7], that is, it is subject to the harmless error test.

§ 1-2   Defense Counsel Perspective.

When Counsel is prepared for the hearing it can act as an excellent vehicle to discover additional evidence, organize for trial, or even to secure a dismissal.

As a discovery device the Preliminary Hearing is second to none. Up until this point in the Criminal Justice Process the only item the Defendant is likely to have in his/her possession is the Criminal Complaint and the Affidavit of Probable Cause.[8] Some defendants become obsessed with this document, convinced that they have discovered the key to unlocking his/her case by the Officer's mistake as to the time, date, or other particulars of the incident. It is important to remind the client that the Affidavit of Probable Cause that prompted the filing of the Complaint is not evidence. No one is convicted of a criminal offense based only on a single piece of paper without supporting

---

[5] *Coleman v. Alabama, 399 U.S. 1, 90 S.Ct. 1999, (1970).* See also
Commonwealth v. Rines, 247 Pa.Super. 429, 372 A.2d 901 (1977);
Commonwealth v. Redshaw, 226 Pa.Super. 534, 323 A.2d 92 (1974).
[6] *P.L.E. Criminal Law 175,* citing *Commonwealth v. Denny, 28 Beaver 189 (1968)* and *Commonwealth v. West, 9 Adams LJ 39 (1967).*
[7] *Commonwealth v. Sawyer, 238 Pa.Super. 213, 357 A.2d 587 (1976)*
[8] See Appendix 1 for a sample Criminal Complaint and Affidavit of Probable Cause

testimony. The evidence comes when the affiant actually testifies before the Court. The affiant often makes corrections, supplies additional information, or makes other changes that can have a significant effect on the Defendant's case.

Defense Counsel can utilize this opportunity to explore issues far afield of the basic assertions made in the Criminal Complaint. Names of other potential witnesses can be uncovered, the Commonwealth's legal theories that tie multiple charges together can be exposed, and potential weaknesses in the Prosecution's case can be laid bare. In this regard, the opportunity for Defense Counsel to secure testimony and information he or she might not normally have access to is unequaled.

The Preliminary Hearing also functions as a superb method for trial preparation. Defense Counsel can almost literally conduct a dry run of trial cross-examination at the Preliminary Hearing. By taking the testimony of the affiant and supporting witnesses, Defense Counsel has locked them into their version of events, and provided a complete record for future review. At the time of trial, Counsel is thus assured that he or she need not ask a question to which the answer is not known.

Of course, there are also those situations where an effective cross-examination can result in a dismissal of some or all of the charges. By competently pursuing all lines of evidence and testimony and citing to applicable law before the District Justice, Counsel may secure a dismissal. Even a partial dismissal of some of the charges facing the client may be desirous.

PRACTICE TIP

Going in to the hearing, Counsel should be sure to discuss with the client the objectives of the hearing. Is it purely an information gathering exercise? Or is there a real possibility of dismissal? Is there a specific charge that the client would like to see dismissed more than the others?

For example, perhaps the client is most concerned about a license suspension due to an offense that applies points to his/her driver's license. Or perhaps the simple assault charge is not a problem but the controlled substances violation would jeopardize the client's job. There are a number of possible combinations that Defense Counsel should explore with the client before the hearing to see if a specific attack on one of the charges is most important to him/her.

---

§ 1-3   Burden of Proof

At the preliminary hearing, the Commonwealth must show the presence of every element necessary to constitute each offense charged and the defendant's complicity in that offense. [9] The standard of proof which the Commonwealth must meet is that of prima facie. Prima Facie is a Latin term which means "at first sight", or "on the first appearance". [10]

---

[9] *Commonwealth v. Lodise. 276 Pa. Super. 484, 419 A.2d 561 (1980).*
[10] "At first sight; on the first appearance; on the face of it; so far as can be judged from the first disclosure; presumably; a fact presumed to be true unless disproved by some evidence to the contrary." Black, Henry Campbell. Black's Law Dictionary, Sixth Edition. St. Paul Minn. West Publishing Co. 1991.

A prima facie case consists of evidence, read in the light most favorable to the Commonwealth, that sufficiently establishes both the commission of a crime and that the accused is probably the perpetrator of that crime.[11] There must simply be a showing of some competent evidence that the defendant committed the offense.[12] Proof beyond a reasonable doubt is not required, but proof which would justify the trial judge submitting the case to the jury at trial is required.[13]

Prima facie standard for preliminary hearing requires that Commonwealth produce evidence of existence of each and every element of crime charged; consequently, absence of evidence as to existence of material element is fatal.[14]

PRACTICE TIP

Although the burden of proof is low at a Preliminary Hearing, the burden is still squarely on the Commonwealth. Counsel should conduct the hearing with an eye toward making the argument during closing that the Commonwealth has failed to meet that burden toward the weakest point of the Commonwealth's case. Take apart the elements of the criminal charge, and focus in on the one element which is not present or is lacking in proof.

Consider, for example, a DUI prosecution which requires the elements of an inability to safely operate a vehicle AND actual physical control of

---

[11] *Commonwealth v. Keller 823 A.2d 1004(Pa.Super.,2003)* citing *Commonwealth v. Fountain, 811 A.2d 24, 25-26 (Pa.Super.2002)*
[12] *Id.*
[13] *Commonwealth v. Wojdak. 502 Pa. 358, 466 A.2d 91 (1983).*
[14] *Commonwealth v. Kelley, 664 A.2d 123, 444 Pa.Super. 377, Super.1995, appeal denied 674 A.2d 1068, 544 Pa. 603.*

> the vehicle. If the Commonwealth has clear evidence of the Defendant's intoxication, such as blowing a .16 on the breathylyzer, but has no eyewitness to support that the Defendant was ever in control of the motor vehicle, then Counsel should stress the lack of prima facie evidence to support the actual physical control element.

§ 1-4 Pre-Preliminary Hearing

Effective representation of the client at the time of the Preliminary Hearing depends on adequate preparation, especially for attorneys new to the process.[15] This means more than simply reviewing the statutes which the client is charged with violating. While by no means exhaustive, the following should be considered at a minimum for effective representation of the client.

§ 1-4.1 Review of the Criminal Complaint and Affidavit of Probable Cause.

The Criminal Complaint and Affidavit of Probable Cause may be the most relevant and powerful documents Defense Counsel can possess at the Preliminary Hearing.[16]

These documents contain the basis for the charges upon which the Defendant has been charged. It gives a brief recitation of the facts from the Affiant's point of view, and the legal basis upon which the Commonwealth relies in criminalizing the Defendant's behaviour. Defense Counsel should consider it

---

[15] See Appendix 2, Preliminary Hearing Checklist
[16] See Appendix 1 for a sample Affidavit of Probable Cause.

imperative that Counsel secure a copy of the Affidavit prior to the Preliminary Hearing to adequately prepare.

The Rules of Criminal Procedure set out the required contents of a Criminal Complaint, and include:[17]

1. The name of the affiant.[18] While usually a police officer,[19] it can also be some other law enforcement personnel, such as a Liquor Control Officer, or even a private citizen if the Complaint is filed as part of a private criminal complaint.[20]
2. The name and address of the defendant, if known.[21]
3. A direct accusation of the alleged criminal conduct,[22] as well as a summary of the facts sufficient to advise the defendant of the nature of the offense charged.[23] This accusation must be made as if under oath, and false accusations are subject to legal penalty.[24] The affiant must sign and date the complaint.[25]

PRACTICE TIP

---

[17] *Pennsylvania Rule of Criminal Procedure 504*
[18] *Pennsylvania Rule of Criminal Procedure 504(1)*
[19] See *Pennsylvania Rule of Criminal Procedure 507* for the procedure regarding approval of Criminal Complaints, an optional rule which may be exercised locally by the District Attorney's Office.
[20] *Pennsylvania Rule of Criminal Procedure 506* for the procedure for approval of private criminal complaints.
[21] *Pennsylvania Rule of Criminal Procedure 504(2)*
[22] *Pennsylvania Rule of Criminal Procedure 504(3)*
[23] *Pennsylvania Rule of Criminal Procedure 504(6)(a)*
[24] *18 Pa.C.S.A. Sec 4904*
[25] *Pennsylvania Rule of Criminal Procedure 504(10)*

> This section, often identified separately as the Affidavit of Probable Cause, is the meat of the Criminal Complaint in that it apprises Defense Counsel of the facts surrounding the charges. It provides an excellent opportunity for Counsel to prepare potential legal arguments or cross-examination questions, and it can be useful to go over this document with the client prior to hearing to determine how his or her version of events differs from that provided by the Affiant.

4. The date when the offense occurred.[26] If the date is an essential element of the crime then it must be noted with specificity. If the date is unknown, or is alleged to have continued for a period of time, then the Affiant is permitted to state that it occurred at some period prior to the expiration of the applicable statute of limitations.

> **PRACTICE TIP**
> The date can be essential in those cases involving statutory rape cases, where the age of the victim is important, or in cases where the criminal statute has changed. Counsel is encouraged to make a review of the charges with an eye toward whether the statuted cited was in effect at the time of the incident, or was enacted in a different form requiring different elements.

---

[26] *Pennsylvania Rule of Criminal Procedure 504(4)*

> An excellent example of this is the DUI law changes which occurred in 2004-2005. Many individuals who committed the crimes prior to the current law being enacted should have been charged with a violation of the old law (*75 PA.C.S.A. 3731*) instead of the new law (*75 PA.C.S.A. 3802*).

5. The location where the offense occurred.[27] Counsel should double check to ensure the offense was committed within the jurisdiction of both the arresting officer, and the Judicial District where charges have been brought.

6. A statement that the acts committed were a violation of the law.[28]

7. A request for criminal laboratory services, if required.[29] For example, for the taking of blood or DNA evidence.

8. A request for an arrest warrant or the issuance of a summons.[30]

Often, the client has been given a copy of this document, and will produce it at the time of the initial consultation. There are times however when Defense Counsel will have to secure it by other means, perhaps the client has misplaced it, or he/she is incarcerated and unable to provide Counsel with a copy prior to the hearing. At such moments, politely contacting the District

---

[27] *Pennsylvania Rule of Criminal Procedure 504(5)*
[28] *Pennsylvania Rule of Criminal Procedure 504(7)*
[29] *Pennsylvania Rule of Criminal Procedure 504(8)*
[30] *Pennsylvania Rule of Criminal Procedure 504(9)*

Justice's Office and sending an Entry of Appearance[31] document should allow Defense Counsel access to the Affidavit. Most District Justices are courteous enough to fax a copy of the Affidavit at Defense Counsel's request, but be advised that not all have the staff to accommodate every request, and Counsel may have to make other arrangements, such as contacting the Officer or the District Attorney's Office to secure same. With the Affidavit in hand Defense Counsel can prepare the cross-examination of the affiant, anticipate any other potential witnesses, and prepare legal arguments.

Counsel is cautioned that the Affidavit is not a magical piece of paper that grants freedom to those who find technical errors within. Even contradictory testimony by the Affiant can be excused by the District Justice because credibility is not an issue at the time of the Preliminary hearing.[32] If testimony conflicts with the Affidavit, it is for a Jury to sort out, not the District Justice. Use the Affidavit as a guide and a preparatory tool, do not rely on it to the exclusion of other methods of effective preparation.

Defense Counsel may find that the client has scoured the Complaint in the hopes of finding some small inconsistency so as to guarantee a dismissal. In such cases kindly point out to the client that a Defendant cannot be discharged and a case cannot be dismissed because of such a defect, unless the defect is prejudicial to the rights of the defendant.[33]

If Counsel does spot such a defect, be aware that it must be raised to the Court's attention prior to the conclusion of the

---

[31] See Appendix 3, Entry of Appearance.
[32] *Commonwealth v. Carmody, 799 A.2d 143 Pa.Super.,2002*, at a preliminary hearing, trial court is not permitted to assess credibility of witness in context of determining prima facie case.
[33] *Pennsylvania Rule of Criminal Procedure 109.*

preliminary hearing.[34] Defense Counsel must establish not only the defect on the record, but also that the Defendant has suffered manifest and palpable harm as a result of the alleged noncompliance.[35]

See for example *Commonwealth v. Slick*, where an amendment of a criminal complaint prior to trial which contained facts arising out of the same set of circumstances and for which the Defendant had sufficient notice to prepare an adequate defense did not constitute such prejudice.[36]

§ 1-4.2 Contact the District Justice's Office

Are there any special procedures Defense Counsel must follow at the time of the Preliminary Hearing? Is it currently scheduled for a "central court" type listing which requires Counsel to request a Preliminary Hearing to be held before one will be scheduled? These and other questions can be quickly answered with a simple call to the District Justice's Office and speaking with his or her clerical staff.

Additionally, Counsel should forward a letter entering his or her appearance on behalf of the client so that notification is forthcoming of continuances or other changes. Many District Justices are courteous enough to contact Defense Counsel directly regarding the concurrence with requests from the Commonwealth, or to reschedule the hearing for a day amenable to both parties.

---

[34] *Pennsylvania Rule of Criminal Procedure 109*, and *Comment*, and *Williams v. Wynder, 2007 U.S. Dist. LEXIS 10473 (D. Pa. 2007)*
[35] *Commonwealth v. Gillmore, 1999 PA Super 43, 726 A.2d 1063 (Pa. Super. Ct. 1999), appeal denied by 560 Pa. 698, 743 A.2d 915 (1999).*
[36] *Commonwealth v. Slick, 432 Pa. Super. 563, 639 A.2d 482, (1994), appeal denied by 538 Pa. 669, 649 A.2d 671, (1994).*

§ 1-4.3 Contact Police Officer

Speaking directly to the Law Enforcement Officer involved can be an effective strategy in reducing the charges prior to the hearing. Many Officers can be reasonable, and if approached ahead of time are willing to come to some kind of an arrangement regarding the withdrawal or dismissal of certain charges. Knowing that they do not have to prepare for an adversarial hearing will sometimes make the Officer more amenable to such a compromise.

In those circumstances where a plea arrangement is not desired, it can still work to Defense Counsel's advantage to contact the Officer. Stereotypically, Police Officers are a confident lot, and many may reveal additional information about the case when Counsel speaks with him/her. He/she may inform Defense Counsel about other pending charges, bring up information about a prior conviction which Counsel was unaware, or reveal the substance of post-arrest investigations. While such information may not be admissible at the time of the Hearing it can prove valuable in formulating a proper strategy.

Linked civil penalties may be another reason to contact the Officer. For example, in DUI refusal cases the Police Officer has to take the active step of submitting the refusal paperwork to the Pennsylvania Department of Transportation, irrespective of the outcome of the Preliminary Hearing. If Counsel can contact the Police Officer ahead of time and indicate that a potential plea could be worked out he/she may agree to withhold submitting the refusal paperwork pending the outcome of the hearing. This may save the client from a significant license suspension; correspondingly, the failure to do so might result in the suspension being imposed. [37]

§ 1-4.4 Contact District Attorney

Determining the intentions of the District Attorney in advance of the hearing is another important preparation technique. Will the District Attorney file additional charges? Does the client qualify for ARD or some other diversionary program?[38] Is the Commonwealth agreeable to a reduction in bail? These and other questions can be addressed in advance by placing a telephone call.

This can sometimes prove difficult depending on the locality. Some jurisdictions do not assign a particular District Attorney to a particular District Justice's Office on a particular schedule, rather, they send whoever is in the Office that day, or whoever is unlucky enough to be available at the time. In such cases, Defense Counsel will be unable to speak with the specific District Attorney who would handle the case.

Even in these cases, Defense Counsel can still uncover important information by speaking to other members of the Office. Speak to the ARD administrator for example, and try to feel out whether the client might qualify for such a program or whether a waiver is required for entry. Speak to the secretaries to determine if they have any updated paperwork on the case which they can forward to Counsel. Even if all Counsel does is put the District Attorney's Office on notice that Defense Counsel

---

[37] See Appendix 4 for a Sample Letter

[38] Admission to an ARD program is not a matter of right, but a privilege. *Commonwealth v. Armstrong, 495 Pa. 506, 512, 434 A.2d 1205, 1208 (1981)* ("Our rules give district attorneys broad discretion to select which crimes and which individuals qualify for diversion into ARD").

will be representing Defendant X at the time of the hearing, the effort will be worthwhile.

§ 1-4.5 Contact Public Defender's Office, or prior counsel

So the District Attorney's Office claims it never enters into a plea or allows ARD if the Hearing isn't waived. But is that policy always enforced? If Defense Counsel is unfamiliar with the jurisdiction and the offices involved, there's no better source than someone who deals with the Commonwealth on a daily basis. For this reason, contact with the Public Defender's Office can be a valuable effort.

When calling, ask to speak to whichever attorney would normally be assigned to the District Justice on the day of the Hearing. Politely inform him/her that Defense Counsel has been retained to represent Defendant X, thus saving an Assistant Public Defender the trouble and expense of having to drive out to the District Justice's Office, and by the way do the District Attorney's really refuse to plea anyone who fights through the Preliminary Hearing?[39]

Sometimes, another private attorney will have already begun representation of the client. Perhaps the client was represented at the Preliminary Arraignment, or consulted with another attorney prior to charges being filed. For whatever reason, the client has now sought out Defense Counsel's services. Regardless of whether or not the client has informed this other attorney his or her services are no longer required, it is good practice to inform this attorney in writing that Defense Counselhas assumed responsibility for the case. This alleviates

---

[39] See Appendix 5, Pre-Hearing letter to Public Defender's Office or prior counsel

the uncertainty as to whether the attorney should still appear and gives Defense Counsel an opportunity to request any evidence which might be in the attorney's possession that could be advantageous to the client.

§ 1-4.6 Secure services of Court Reporter

As mentioned in other portions of this guide, the services of a Court Reporter to transcribe the testimony will prove invaluable as the case progresses. Defense Counsel will never regret having a transcript of the testimony elicited at the Preliminary Hearing.

PRACTICE TIP

Develop a relationship with a local court reporter who is reliable and accurate. Good reporters can be counted on to provide transcripts in a timely manner, and are often willing to show up on a moment's notice (although most appreciate as much warning as possible). Always be sure to include the anticipated cost of the transcript in the initial fee quote to the client – do not count on the client to pay for the transcript or appearance on his or her own. Nothing can breed bad feelings between an attorney and court reporter faster than an unpaid bill for a transcript which was produced and forwarded to Defense Counsel in expectation of payment. Make paying the Court Reporter a priority and a mutually beneficial relationship can be guaranteed.

If Defense Counsel is visiting an unfamiliar county then he or she should begin by consulting the local court reporters for a referral. Failing that, contact the public defender's office or the bar association.

§ 1-4.7 Prepare relevant questions

While reviewing the Affidavit of Probable Cause and the client's statements to Counsel, try to determine which factual issues haven't been addressed. For example, why didn't the Officer mention anything about the other people in the house at the time of the drug arrest? Who are these potential witnesses?

While it might seem redundant, asking the Officer questions which have already been answered in the Affidavit of Probable Cause can be important. The last thing Defense Counsel want is to base the entire suppression argument on a line in the Affidavit about when the Officer read the Defendant his/her Miranda rights, only to have the Officer remember things differently at the time of a suppression hearing. Asking the Officer to repeat the factual allegation at the time of the Hearing locks the testimony down, and makes it easier to call him or her on it at the time of a suppression hearing.

> **PRACTICE TIP**
> Defense Counsel should eventually reach a level where which questions are relevant in any particular matter becomes second nature. This level can take years of practice however, during which Counsel is still required to provide competent legal services. To that end, Counsel may consider writing out beforehand all questions which come to mind for the cross-

> examination of known witnesses such as law
> enforcement personnel.
>
> While this solution is not ideal, the
> alternative, missing relevant questions, is a worse
> outcome for the client.

When using the Preliminary Hearing as an information gathering exercise it is more important to ask a full slate of questions that may reveal other information than it is to impress anyone with Defense Counsel's skills as a cross-examiner. The transcript does not record the fact that Counsel read each question from a pre-set list. Not having asked a relevant question at the Preliminary Hearing can be disastrous at trial.

Even when using a list of questions Counsel should be sure that the questions are answered fully and be prepared for follow up if necessary. If Counsel is truly clueless about which questions to ask in a particular prosecution, there is no better guide than the transcripts of a prior hearing. Counsel in a firm with other criminal defense attorneys should ask if there was a previous case handled with a similar fact pattern and use the transcript from that case as a starting point.

§ 1-4.8 Prepare for likely legal issues

Does it appear the Commonwealth has zero evidence regarding the client's intent to commit the crime in question? Is there a significant issue regarding the probable cause to stop and search the Defendant? Prepare for this and other legal issues by doing some preliminary research. Remember that literally thousands of Preliminary Hearings have been held across the Commonwealth on exactly these charges in the past. If Defense

INTRODUCTION

Counsel notices a pattern about how to attack the legal basis for the charges, there is a good possibility it will come up again.

Preliminary research also allows Defense Counsel to prepare for issue spotting during testimony. Something may come out during testimony that wasn't present in the Affidavit of Probable Cause but that could have a significant effect on a possible suppression motion. Knowing that the issue exists will allow Counsel to ask follow up questions to narrow in on that issue and preserve the testimony for later hearing.

§ 1-4.9 Prepare the Client

Some Defendants expect that if given a few minutes to explain the situation, the charges will have to be dismissed. They may be convinced that the Officer or witness is mistaken or being deceitful about a particular part of the case, and that if they could only reveal his or her side of the story to the Court, that the charges would be immediately dismissed. In such cases explain to the client that his or her testimony is unlikely to be presented at the time of the Preliminary Hearing. Credibility is not an issue so the Judge has to proceed as if the witnesses for the Commonwealth are being truthful. Except in those extremely rare cases where a simple explanation really can rebut a prima facie level of evidence, the client should not testify. It opens him or her up to cross-examination, limits what he or she can say at trial, and will aid the Commonwealth substantially more than it will the Defendant.

Also explain to the client proper decorum in the Courtroom. While it is true that the Courts of District Justice are less formal than Court of Common Pleas, the Judge is still an elected official with judicial powers. When in doubt, give just as much deference to the District Justice as one would to any formal judicial officer. Remind the client that the Magisterial District Justice may hold him or her in contempt if their behaviour is disrespectful or otherwise obstructs the administration of justice.[40]

PRACTICE TIP

Clients are often understandably nervous, confused, or angry at the time of the Preliminary Hearing, especially if witness testimony which they view as false is presented. To prevent the client from acting out or enraging the Court, Counsel should have a clear conversation with the client before the hearing. Explain that everything said is being recorded by the Court Reporter so respectful behaviour is required. Whenever I fear the client will have trouble controlling his or her emotions I give the client a blank legal pad and instruct him or her to make notes of the testimony and to write any questions which occur to them during the case. This helps to focus the client's attention and keeps him or her from having an emotional outburst.

Finally, a formal retainer letter, setting forth the basis of the representation is essential. In the letter, Defense Counsel should set forth the terms of the attorney client relationship, with particular attention to whether or not the representation is limited to just the Preliminary Hearing, and what the expected costs will be.

---

[40] *Pennsylvania Rule of Criminal Procedure 140 (a)(1)*

2

LEGAL BASIS FOR THE
PRELIMINARY HEARING

21

Pennsylvania is far from a homogenous set of Criminal Procedure Rules, and while it has made significant strides in recent years there still remain many local rules with which Counsel should be intimately familiar. It is entirely possible that such local rules may come into conflict with the Rules of Criminal Procedure, often by the creation of a new rule or statute. Localities may be slow to adopt the new standard, so counsel should be ever vigilant that the local procedures do not violate Commonwealth-wide rules, or prejudice the rights of his or her client. Fortunately, it is clear that any conflict must be resolved in favour of the Commonwealth-wide rules.[41]

§ 2-1 Magisterial District Justice Authority, Venue and Jurisdiction

Magisterial District Justices have authority to hear cases arising within the physical confines of the Magisterial District for which he or she is elected.[42]

When the location where the criminal activity occurred is unknown, the proceedings may be brought before any Magisterial District Justice within the entire County.[43] When the criminal activity occurs in more than one magisterial district, yet still within the same County, then the proceedings may be filed in any of those Magisterial Districts.[44] There are also those circumstances where the alleged criminal activity occurred in more than one county. In such cases, any affected Magisterial District Justice may serve as the home for the filing of criminal

---

[41] *Pennsylvania Rule of Criminal Procedure 105(b)*

[42] *Pennsylvania Rule of Criminal Procedure 131(a),* and *Rule 130(a)*

[43] *Pennsylvania Rule of Criminal Procedure 130(a)(1),* or within 100 yards of the boundary between two or more neighbouring Magisterial Districts. *Rule 130(a)(5)*

[44] *Pennsylvania Rule of Criminal Procedure 130(a)(2)*

charges.[45] The decision as to where venue lies is a decision to be made initially by the Officers for the Commonwealth.[46] Venue may be transferred by the Officers for the Commonwealth to any other Magisterial District Justice having venue under the rules of Criminal Procedure.[47]

The Defendant has a right to object to the venue of a Magisterial District Justice or to the transfer of a preliminary hearing from one Magisterial District to another.[48] Such an objection must be brought before the Court of Common Pleas prior to the completion of the Preliminary Hearing.[49] The standard for an objection to venue is that a Defendant must show substantial prejudice will result if the proceeding is allowed to continue.[50]

In those circumstances where a Defendant is successful in challenging the venue of a Magisterial District to hear the case, the result is not a dismissal, but rather a transfer to the proper Magisterial District as directed by the Court of Common Pleas.[51]

Note that venue is different from jurisdiction. While venue is an argument that may be waived by a failure to raise the issue prior to completion of a preliminary hearing, the jurisdiction of the offense may be raised at any time during the

---

[45] *Pennsylvania Rule of Criminal Procedure 130(a)(3)*

[46] *Pennsylvania Rule of Criminal Procedure 130 (comment)*

[47] *Pennsylvania Rule of Criminal Procedure 130(b)*

[48] *Pennsylvania Rule of Criminal Procedure 134(a) and Rule 134 (comment)*

[49] *Pennsylvania Rule of Criminal Procedure 134(a)*

[50] *Pennsylvania Rule of Criminal Procedure 134(b)* and see *Appendix 4* for a sample Objection to Venue

[51] *Pennsylvania Rule of Criminal Procedure 134(c)*

proceedings, even post-conviction, [52] and even after the entrance of a guilty plea.[53]

Jurisdiction is only acquired when the crime is committed within the county in which the Court sits, and the Defendant is properly before the court, having been "confronted by the Commonwealth with a formal and specific accusation of the crimes charged."[54]

Once the case has progressed past the preliminary hearing stage, the rules further provide for the transfer of criminal proceedings as provided in rules *555(a)(1) and (2)*. The proceedings in such cases may be transferred by written agreement of all parties filed with the Clerk of Courts of each district, including multiple District Attorneys or Defense Counsel.[55]

If Defense Counsel does not agree to the transfer, the Attorneys for the Commonwealth are to file their written agreement with the Clerk of Courts[56] and provide 10 days within which Defense Counsel may file an objection.[57] The Court of Common Pleas may schedule a hearing or otherwise promptly dispose of the objection.[58] Once transferred, the case proceeds according to all applicable rules of procedure[59], with the note that any rulings, orders, or other determinations made prior to

---

[52] *Commonwealth v. Ziegler, 251 Pa.Super. 147, 150, 380 A.2d 420, 422 (1977),*

[53] *Commonwealth v. Mangum, 231 Pa.Super. 162, 164, 332 A.2d 467, 468 (1974)* and *Commonwealth v. Borris, 280 Pa.Super. 369, 421 A.2d 767 (1980)*

[54] *Commonwealth v. Little, 455 Pa. 163, 168, 314 A.2d 270, 273 (1974).*

[55] *Pennsylvania Rule of Criminal Procedure 555(b)(1).*, See *Appendix 9* for a sample written agreement to transfer

[56] *Pennsylvania Rule of Criminal Procedure 555(b)(2)*

[57] *Pennsylvania Rule of Criminal Procedure 555(b)(2) and (d)(1),* See *Appendix 10* for a sample objection to transfer the proceedings

[58] *Pennsylvania Rule of Criminal Procedure 555(d)(2).*

[59] *Pennsylvania Rule of Criminal Procedure 555(f)*

transfer are binding on the new forum.[60] Any outstanding costs, with the exception of bail related costs, are due and owing in the transfer district.[61]

For example, if discovery has been initiated, and the judge in the transferring judicial district has ordered or denied disclosure, this order would be binding on the judge and parties in the transfer judicial district.[62]

§ 2-2 Time and Location of the Preliminary Hearing

Preliminary Hearings following the Preliminary Arraignment of a Defendant must be held no earlier than three days or more than ten days after the Preliminary Arraignment.[63] The hearing can be continued for cause, or set for an earlier date with the consent of all parties.[64]

In those cases where the proceedings are instituted by the filing of a summons, the date for the Preliminary Hearing must be not less than twenty days from the date of mailing of the summons, unless by the consent of all parties.[65]

Preliminary hearings are to be held publically.[66] Preliminary Hearings are "court proceedings", subject to the open courts provision in the Commonwealth and Federal Constitutions, and the public may not be denied access to

---

[60] *Pennsylvania Rule of Criminal Procedure (f)(3)*
[61] *Pennsylvania Rule of Criminal Procedure (f)(4)* and *Comment.*
[62] See *Commonwealth v. Starr, 664 A.2d 1326 (Pa. 1995),* concerning the coordinate jurisdiction rule and the law of the case doctrine. *Pennsylvania Rule of Criminal Procedure 555, Comment.*
[63] *Pennsylvania Rule of Criminal Procedure 540(F)(1)*
[64] *Pennsylvania Rule of Criminal Procedure 540(F)(1)(a)* and *(b)*
[65] *Pennsylvania Rule of Criminal Procedure 510(A)*
[66] *Pennsylvania Rule of Criminal Procedure 131(a)(3)*

them.[67] However, the taking or transmission of photographs or video recordings is prohibited.[68]

Hearings are usually held in the Magisterial District Justice's office, or some other central Court or facility designated by the President Judge of the County.[69] While preliminary arraignments may be held using some form of teleconferencing communication technology,[70] preliminary hearings constitute a critical stage of the proceedings, and may not be held using such methods.[71]

The President Judge may set a central Court for preliminary Hearings.[72] Be aware that many times the Central Court is only a listing for waivers, and that if the client intends to enter a defense or hold a hearing the Judge will continue the hearing from central court to a time certain. In such cases Counsel can often save the time and expense of having to appear twice by contacting the District Justice's office ahead of time with an intent to defend.[73]

This also provides that the President Judge may set a special time and place for particular classes of Defendants, for example, those who are presently incarcerated.[74] Such a proceeding might be scheduled at a location at or near the correctional facility, and need not be within the confines of the Magisterial District where the incident occurred.[75]

The President Judge is also empowered to temporarily reassign the coverage of any Magisterial District Justice when

---

[67] *In re Petition of Daily Item, 310 Pa. Super. 222 (1983)*

[68] *Rule 112(A)(1) and (2)*

[69] *Rule 131(a)(1)*

[70] *Rule 131(a)(2)*

[71] *Rule 540*

[72] *Rule 131(b)*

[73] See *Appendix 3* for sample Entry of Appearance and Notice to Defend.

[74] *Rule 131, Comment*

[75] *Rule 130(a)(5)*

such assignment is needed,[76] such as to insure fair and impartial proceedings,[77] conduct a preliminary hearing following the dismissal of charges under *Pennsylvania Rule of Criminal Procedure 544(b)*,[78] or as otherwise required for the efficient administration of justice.[79]

Defense Counsel and the Commonwealth are permitted to file for such a temporary assignment when the fairness and impartiality of the proceedings require same.[80] Such a hearing must be filed at the Court of Common Pleas and reasonable notice and an opportunity to respond shall be provided to all the parties.[81] To justify the reassignment, a showing of bias by the judge sought to be replaced, such as would preclude a fair and impartial proceeding must be demonstrated.[82]

§ 2-3 Notice and Continuances

The District Justice is required to provide written notice of the hearing to the Defendant, the Defendant's attorney, and the Attorney for the Commonwealth.[83] Notice may be provided by personal service or by first class mail.[84]

Continuances of a scheduled preliminary hearing may be granted for cause shown.[85] The District Justice is required to

---

[76] *Rule 132*
[77] *Rule 132(a)(2)*
[78] *Rule 132(a)(3)*
[79] *Rule 132(a)(4)*
[80] *Rule 132(c)*
[81] *Rule 132(c) and Comment.*
[82] *Commonwealth v. Kline, 521 Pa. 281, 555 A.2d 892, (1989)*, criticized by *Commonwealth v. Shoop, 420 Pa. Super. 606, 617 A.2d 351, (1992)*. See *Appendix 10* for a sample Objection to Transfer, and *Appendix 11* for a sample Motion to Reassign.
[83] *Rule 542(e)(2)(a)*
[84] *Rule 542(e)(2)(b) and (c)*
[85] *Rule 542(e)*

note on the transcript the granting of the continuance as well as the grounds upon which the continuance is granted[86], the identity of the party requesting the continuance for purposes of *Rule 600* considerations[87], and the rescheduled date and time of the hearing, as well as the reasons that date was chosen.[88] Commonly, District Justices hold criminal hearings on a regular schedule, and a rescheduled hearing to the next available date is not unreasonable.

A request for a continuance by a Defendant to obtain counsel is sufficient justification for the grant of same,[89] however, the computation of the time period involved will be held against the Defendant for *Rule 600* purposes.[90]

The District Justice may refuse to grant a continuance, even in cases where counsel has only recently been retained. The question in such a situation is whether any specified harm from such a denial is demonstrated.[91] Additionally, a denial is permitted even where the Defendant requests additional time to secure the services of a Court Reporter where there is no evidence Defendant was unable to arrange for such services, and provided that Defendant's counsel was present and permitted to take notes.[92]

---

[86] *Rule 542(e)(1)(a)*
[87] *Rule 542(e)(1)(b)*
[88] *Rule 542(e)(1)(c)*
[89] See *Appendix 13* for sample letter requesting continuance
[90] *Commonwealth v. Wade, 380 A.2d 782, 475 Pa. 399, Sup.1977.*
[91] *Commonwealth v. Palmer, 417 A.2d 229, 273 Pa.Super. 184, Super.1979.*
[92] *Commonwealth v. Gelormo, 475 A.2d 765, 327 Pa.Super. 219, Super.1984.*

§ 2-4   Procedure at hearing

Preliminary hearings in the Commonwealth of Pennsylvania are procedurally directed by *Rule of Criminal Procedure 542*, which provides that an Attorney for the Commonwealth may appear at a preliminary hearing and take charge of the prosecution.[93] This relieves the Complainant or Police Officer of the duty to prosecute. See *Rule 542(b)* for the procedures involved when no attorney for the Commonwealth appears. Defense Counsel should note that the appearance of the District Attorney at the time of the Preliminary Hearing is not always guaranteed. Depending on the seriousness of the charges, and the particular procedures in the jurisdiction, Defense Counsel may only be facing off with a State Police Trooper, or even a municipal police officer. Regardless, Counsel should not underestimate his or her opponent, and should prepare legal arguments and cross-examination questions to the best of one's ability.

The District Attorney, or the affiant in his or her absence, may make recommendations to the Court concerning whether the Defendant should be discharged or the case bound over for court following the presentation of evidence.[94]

At the time of the Preliminary Hearing the District Justice is faced with determining whether the Commonwealth has introduced sufficient prima facie evidence to support the charges in question.[95] In a preliminary hearing, the court has the power to "bind the charges over" which would result in a trial on the merits of the evidence at the Court of Common Pleas, or

---

[93] *Rule 542(a)(1).*
[94] *Rule 542(a)(2).*
[95] *Rule 543(b)*

dismiss the charges altogether as lacking the elements necessary to go to trial.[96]

There is a clear distinction between a preliminary hearing and a criminal trial. While a trial determines guilt or innocence, the preliminary hearing is held primarily to prevent the detention of a person for a crime that was never committed or of a crime with which there is no evidence of his connection. The question at a preliminary hearing is not whether there is sufficient evidence to prove the defendant guilty beyond a reasonable doubt; rather, the question is whether the prosecution must be dismissed because there is nothing to indicate that the defendant is connected with a crime.[97]

If the charges are found to be without basis of prima facie evidence of the Defendant's guilt, then the complaint should be dismissed.[98] Note that the District Justice may allow a continuance on behalf of the Commonwealth to supplement with additional evidence if good cause for such a continuance can be shown.[99]

---

[96] *Id.*
[97] *Commonwealth v. Rick. 366 A.2d 302 (Pa.Com.Pl.1988)*
[98] *Rule 543(e).*
[99] *Rule 543(e)*

3

DEFENDANT'S RIGHTS AND RESPONSIBILITIES

The Defendant is required to be present at the preliminary hearing and has certain enumerated rights at that time.[100]

§ 3-1 Right to Be Represented by Counsel.[101]

This may be the single most important item of preparation the defendant can do.[102] The burden is then put on Defense Counsel's shoulders to ensure the client's rights are protected, and that the evidence is examined in a thorough manner.

The United States Supreme Court has delineated the advantages of a lawyer's assistance at a preliminary hearing.

> "First, the lawyer's skilled examination and cross-examination of witnesses may expose fatal weaknesses in the State's case that may lead the magistrate to refuse to bind the accused over.
>
> Second, in any event, the skilled interrogation of witnesses by an experienced lawyer can fashion a vital impeachment tool for use in cross-examination of the State's witnesses at the trial, or preserve testimony favorable to the accused of a witness who does not appear at the trial.
>
> Third, trained counsel can more effectively discover the case the State has

---

[100] *Rule 542(c)*

[101] *Rule 542(c)(1)*

[102] To ensure Counsel is correctly docketed as representative for the Defendant an appearance should be entered at the earliest possible moment. See *Appendix 3* for a sample letter entering Counsel's appearance.

against his client and make possible the preparation of a proper defense to meet that case at the trial.

Fourth, counsel can also be influential at the preliminary hearing in making effective arguments for the accused on such matters as the necessity for an early psychiatric examination or bail."[103] [Structure emphasized]

§ 3-2 Right to be present.[104]

Of course, the Defendant has the right to appear on his or her own behalf so as to ensure the proper exercise of the remaining rights. A criminal defendant has the right to be present at all critical stages of criminal proceedings.[105]

Pennsylvania Rule of Criminal Procedure 119(a)1 currently prohibits the use of two-way simultaneous audio-visual communication in Preliminary Hearings. The client has the absolute right to be present, absent some evidence of flight or fraudulent concealment of his or her location. See *Rule 543(d)* for information on hearings held in absentia.

There are those cases of course, where the client will fail to appear for the preliminary hearing. If possible, it is recommended that Counsel seek a continuance of the hearing until such time as the client is available. Any good faith reason as to why the client failed to appear will likely provide for the continuance, and prevent the entry of an arrest warrant.[106] In those cases where Defense Counsel cannot establish good cause

---

[103] *Coleman v. Alabama, 399 U.S. 1, 90 S.Ct. 1999, (1970)*
[104] *Rule 542(c)*
[105] *Commonwealth v. Flores, 2007 PA Super 87, 921 A.2d 517 (2007).*
Preliminary hearing is an "important stage".
[106] *Rule 542(d)(2)*

for the client's absence, the Magisterial District Justice is empowered to hold the hearing in his or her absence[107] and hold the case for court if a prima facie case is established.[108]

There may be circumstances where the client is truthfully unable to appear, and regardless, Counsel wishes the hearing to proceed in his or her absence. Defense Counsel must contact the Magisterial District Justice, the District Attorney and the Arresting Officer well in advance to ensure same is acceptable, and that bail going forward will not be an issue. The Magisterial District Justice may require a signed notice of waiver of the hearing to prevent the entry of a bench warrant.

§ 3-3   Right to make a record of the proceedings.[109]

A transcript of the proceedings is absolutely crucial to the client's case. The transcript locks parties in to testimony and establishes likely legal issues.

> "Defense Counsel should be familiar with the [affiant's] preliminary hearing testimony and have at the ready the transcript of such testimony in case the officer's trial testimony is inconsistent with that of the preliminary hearing. This is fertile territory for cross-examination."[110]

While it is always recommended to secure the services of a professional Court Reporter, preferably a local service, if no such reporter can be obtained Defense Counsel may make an

---

[107] *Rule 542(d)(3)(a)*
[108] *Rule 542(d)(3)(b)*
[109] *Rule 542(c)(3)*
[110] Wile and Werlinsky. Pennsylvania Driving Under the Influence, Vol. 10. Thomson West. 2005.

audio recording of the hearing and have it transcribed at a later date. However, before using a recording device check with the District Justice, and be courteous enough to inform all parties when the recording begins and ends.

Defense Counsel will always be able to refer to this transcript later in the proceedings in order contradict testimony, arrange for subsequent discovery, or otherwise preserve the record of the testimony presented at the time of the Preliminary Hearing.[111]

§ 3-4   Right to cross-examine witnesses and inspect physical evidence offered against the defendant.[112]

The reason Defense Counsel has been retained is for this portion of the hearing – the cross-examination. Counsel should use the Affidavit of Probable Cause, the information supplied by the Defendant and any other resources at his or her disposal to begin a careful, deliberate, and methodical cross-examination of the affiant or witness. This is one of the few times an attorney can be permitted to ask questions he or she doesn't know the answers to. Consider this like the deposition conducted in a civil case; Counsel's objective may not be a specific line of questioning designed to convince someone of the client's innocence, rather it is a wide net to secure as much evidence and testimony as possible for later use.

---

[111] *Commonwealth v. Stasko, 471 Pa. 373, 370 A.2d 350 (1977); Commonwealth v. Clarkson, 438 Pa. 523, 265 A.2d 802 (1970).* Providing for use at trial of prior testimony taken before a court of record.
[112] 542(c)(2)

How wide can this net be?[113] The Commonwealth may sometimes object to a line of questioning as beyond the scope of the Preliminary Hearing. Unfortunately, such objections will often be sustained by the District Justice. It is a difficult balance to ask as many and as varied questions as possible while still remaining inside the scope of questioning allowed by the Court.[114] In these cases, it may be better to move on to another aspect of the case and then attempt to return to the information sought at another time and from another angle.

§ 3-5 Right to call witnesses on the defendant's own behalf other than witnesses to the defendant's good reputation only, and the right to offer evidence on the defendant's own behalf, and testify.[115]

Of course, the Defense is permitted to attempt to rebut the evidence and testimony of the Commonwealth by offering evidence of testimony of its own. This raises an important question. When, if ever, is it appropriate for the Defendant to testify?

---

[113] "While it is true that the focus of a preliminary hearing is narrower than that of a trial, we are not persuaded that the difference requires exclusion of the testimony taken at such a hearing. Our basic concern is for the reliability of the testimony which was elicited in the preliminary hearing, and we do not feel that its reliability is affected by the scope or focus of the proceeding. It would certainly be more desirable to have the witness present at trial, but it would be vastly less desirable to exclude such evidence altogether." *Commonwealth v. Clarkson, supra 438 Pa. at 525, 265 A.2d at 803,*

[114] Counsel should be permitted enough latitude in the examination and cross-examination of witnesses so as to enable him to "expose fatal weaknesses in the State's case that may lead ... to [the refusal] to bind the accused over ... [and] fashion a vital impeachment tool for use in cross-examination of the State's witnesses at the trial." *Commonwealth v. Redshaw. 226 Pa. Super. 534, 323 A.2d 92 (1974).*

[115] *542(c)(3) and (4)*

Considering how little impact such testimony is likely to have, and weighed against the overwhelmingly negative consequences that can result if the Defendant is unprepared for cross-examination, it usually makes little sense to testify. Unless there is some clear issue of fact that the defendant can clear up immediately and unequivocally, there is no upside to presenting such testimony. Anything he or she does say will be scrutinized by the District Attorney's Office in much the same way Defense Counsel will be scrutinizing the Police Officer's Testimony prior to the time of trial.

However, calling third party witnesses may have great value to the client. Such witnesses are normally only permitted to testify in order to negate the existence of the Commonwealth's prima facie case, not merely for the purpose of discovering the Commonwealth's case.[116] Defense Counsel should balance these two measures to ensure that as much information is gleaned from potential trial witnesses as possible.

To ensure the attendance of such witnesses, District Justices are permitted to issue subpoenas to testify or produce documents upon request of either the Commonwealth or the Defendant.[117] These witnesses must be sworn under penalty of perjury.[118] This provides a great resource to Defense Counsel, especially when combined with a full and accurate transcription of such testimony. This ensures that the witnesses' testimony is preserved and made available for further suppression motions, discovery, or trial preparation.

The contents of a subpoena in a criminal case, whether at the Preliminary hearing or otherwise, must contain the identity of the person being subpoenaed. Additionally, the date, time and

---

[116] *Rule 543 Comment,*

[117] *Rule 545(a),* and see *Appendix 11* for a Sample Subpoena Letter

[118] *Rule 545(b)*

place where the person is to appear must be specified. The subpoena may identify any items or documents to be produced at that time. The subpoena request must also state on whose behalf the witness is being subpoenaed, as well as the identity and contact information of counsel.[119]

A subpoena may be used not only at trial, but at any other stage of the proceedings, including preliminary hearings.[120]

§ 3-6 Right to an interpreter

It is the policy of the Commonwealth to protect the rights of persons who are not native English speakers, or who because of impairment are unable to understand or communicate adequately in English, whenever such a person appears in a judicial proceeding.[121] This program is is set up by the Administrative Office of Pennsylvania Courts.[122] The AOPC currently maintains a list of interpreters in various languages who are certified for Court use throughout the Commonwealth.[123]

In a criminal matter, the Defendant and any witnesses he intends to call on his behalf may have such translation services provided to him with the costs borne by the County.[124] The statutory language provides that translation services are of right to a party at any appearance in court or whenever involved in judicial proceedings.[125]

---

[119] *Rule 107*

[120] *Rule 107 (comment)*

[121] *42 Pa.C.S. § 4401*

[122] *42 Pa.C.S. § 4411*

[123] http://www.courts.state.pa.us/NR/rdonlyres/42C834EA-65AC-40B2-B3FE-732C821D3F2C/0/InterpreterRoster.pdf

[124] *42 Pa.C.S. § 4416*

[125] *42 Pa.C.S. § 4401*

The appointment may be made upon request of the Defendant or sua sponte by the Court.[126] In those circumstances where a certified interpreter is not immediately available, the Court may appoint an otherwise qualified person to serve as interpreter.[127]

A Defendant has a similar right to interpretative services when he or she is deaf pursuant to *42 Pa.C.S. § 4431*

Defense Counsel should consider whether an interpreter is necessary at the time of the Preliminary Hearing. Requesting an interpreter will often delay the proceedings, so such a request should be made as early as possible.[128]

PRACTICE TIP

Dealing bilingually with clients can present additional challenges to Defense Counsel. Chief among these is to ensure the client understands the role of Counsel in the proceedings. To accomplish this, Counsel may wish to have an interpreter at the initial consult, and to translate the retainer agreement into the client's primary language.

While it is permissible with the permission of the Court and the Commonwealth to have a friend or family member translate for the client at the Preliminary Hearing, this is not ideal. Perhaps most importantly, Counsel should not attempt to act as the interpreter, no matter how familiar with the client's primary tongue he

---

[126] *42 Pa.C.S. § 4412*
[127] *42 Pa.C.S. § 4412 (b)(1)* and *(b)(2)*
[128] See *Appendix 26* for a sample request to the issuing authority for a request for interpretive services.

or she may be. This creates a potential for conflict if Counsel is at all mistaken in his or her translation to client. Attempting to interpret the proceedings at the time when Counsel should be preparing legal objections and questions for cross examination is a difficult prospect, and the translation services should be left to a qualified professional.

Counsel may also wish to consider having the Preliminary Hearing transcript translated for the client after the hearing and in preparation of trial.

4

LEGAL ISSUES AT THE PRELIMINARY HEARING

The Preliminary Hearing is not the proper forum for complex legal argument. Many suppression issues, for example, will not be addressed. Defense Counsel should be prepared to bring such issues to the attention of the Court of Common Pleas Judges if the charges are bound over for Court. Regardless, Defense Counsel should be prepared to ask the relevant questions and make appropriate legal arguments.

This accomplishes two goals. First, it secures testimony that locks the affiant in and prevents surprises at suppression hearings or at trial. Second, it ensures anyone reviewing Defense Counsel's performance that the performance was competent and professional.

By securing the testimony of the affiant Defense Counsel has created a template that can lead to further research on the issues and prepare for pretrial hearings. Regardless of whether or not the affiant appears and testifies at the time of those hearings, Defense Counsel will have a transcript that can be presented to the Court with the relevant portions highlighted. Fit this into the facts of a case previously decided by an appellate Court and Defense Counsel will have a much easier time convincing the Judge that Defense's legal analysis is correct.

Also, should someone be reviewing Counsel's performance at the Preliminary Hearing, he or she will be better able to appreciate the effort that went into the case preparation. This isn't just for those in private practice reporting to a firm's Partner. Consider that a client often receives a copy of the transcript; the legal argument at the time of the hearing will show him or her that Counsel takes the case seriously. Further, although it does not benefit Counsel directly, should the client decide to proceed on the case with another attorney, even one outside of the firm, there is now a primer on possible suppression issues. An attorney's ethical obligations to his or her client do not necessarily end just because the client has secured the services of alternate counsel.

PRACTICE TIP

Counsel should always keep the state of the case prepared as if another attorney will be taking over at any time. This promotes organization of Counsel's file, and also ensures that the client's interests are protected should some unforeseen circumstance necessitate Counsel's withdrawal or removal. There is little more frustrating for replacement Counsel than to have to decipher pages of handwritten scrawl or secretive notations to understand prior Counsel's legal theories.

Keeping the file orderly is a service to the client, to potential new Counsel, and to current Counsel's Office Manager and should not be neglected.

Raising the legal issues at a Preliminary Hearing could come in handy should there ever be a dispute as to the competency of representation. Should Defense Counsel have to sue the client for non-payment of fees he/she may claim that Counsel "didn't do anything to justify the fee". Having the transcript, with thoughtful legal argument included, can go a long way to defeating that claim.

§ 4-1   Competency vs. Credibility

Credibility is defined as the "worthiness of belief" of a witness.[129] The Standard Pennsylvania Criminal Jury Instruction on Credibility reads as follows:

> "1. While you are deciding the facts of this case, you will have to judge the credibility and weight of the testimony and other evidence. By credibility, I mean the truthfulness and accuracy.
>
> 2. When you judge the credibility and weight of a witness's testimony, you are deciding whether you believe all, part, or none of the witness's testimony and how important that testimony is. Use your understanding of human nature and your common sense. Observe each witness as he or she testifies. Be alert for anything in the witness's own testimony or behavior or for anything in the other evidence that might help you judge the truthfulness, accuracy, and weight of his or her testimony."
> *Pa. SSJI (Crim) 2.04*

---

[129] "Worthiness of belief; that quality in a witness which renders his evidence worthy of belief. After the competence of a witness is allowed, the consideration of his credibility arises, and not before." Black, Henry Campbell. Black's Law Dictionary, Sixth Edition. St. Paul Minn. West Publishing Co. 1991.
Competency – "...Competency differs from credibility. The former is a question which arises before considering the evidence given by the witness; the latter concerns the degree of credit to be given to his testimony... Competency is for the court; credibility for the jury." Id.

Pennsylvania case law has made it clear that Defense Counsel may not attack the credibility of a Commonwealth witness at the time of the Preliminary hearing.[130] While Counsel is encouraged to explore any issues relating to the truthfulness of a witnesses testimony, be aware that the District Justice may attempt to severely curtail this kind of cross-examination.

However, the competency of a witness is relevant anytime a witness testifies. Competency is the mental capacity of a witness to perceive the occurrence accurately and to be able to express him or herself coherently.[131] The General rule in Pennsylvania is that every witness is presumed competent to testify.[132] However, this presumption can be attacked using several methods, and the witness can be disqualified if, due to the mental condition or immaturity, the witness is or was incapable of perceiving accurately,[133] unable to express him or herself so as to be understood either directly or through a qualified interpreter,[134] has an impaired memory,[135] or does not sufficiently understand the duty to tell the truth.[136]

The relevant inquiry on competency is whether the witness: (1) has the capacity to observe or perceive the occurrence with a substantial degree of accuracy; (2) has the ability to remember the event which was observed or perceived;

---

[130] "[M]agistrate is precluded from considering the credibility of a witness who is called upon to testify during the preliminary hearing." *Liciaga v. Court of Common Pleas, 523 Pa. 258, 263 (Pa. 1989)*, citing *Commonwealth v. Wojdak, 502 Pa. 359, 466 A.2d 991 (1983); Commonwealth v. Hampton, 462 Pa. 322, 341 A.2d 101 (1975)*.

[131] *Pa.R.Evidence 601, Commonwealth v. D.J.A., 2001 PA Super 204, (Pa. Super. Ct. 2001)*, substituted opinion at *2002 PA Super 176, 800 A.2d 965, (Pa. Super. Ct. 2002)*.

[132] *Pennsylvania Rule of Evidence 601(a)*

[133] *Pennsylvania Rule of Evidence 601(b)1*

[134] *Pennsylvania Rule of Evidence 601(b)2*

[135] *Pennsylvania Rule of Evidence 601(b)3*

[136] *Pennsylvania Rule of Evidence 601(b)4*

(3) has the ability to understand questions and to communicate intelligent answers about the occurrence; and (4) has a consciousness of the duty to speak the truth.[137]

The party challenging competency bears the burden of proving incompetency by clear and convincing evidence.[138] While drug use is relevant to a determination of competency, it does not per se reduce a witness to incompetency.[139]

To explore this issue at the Preliminary Hearing, be sure to cross-examine the witness on his or her ability to testify, to understand the questions being asked, and the requirement to tell the truth. Inquire as to recent drug or alcohol use, and what effect that drug use has had on the person. Does the witness speak English adequately to be responsive to questioning? Remember that the transcript being produced may not pick up on the physical manifestations of the witness' difficulties, so it is important for Counsel to make clear on the record if there are audio or visual clues as to the witness' incapacity.

Is the witness nervous? Ask him or her about it directly, "You seem rather nervous Mr. Regal. Is there some issue which would prevent you from telling the truth here today?" Is the witness shaking uncontrollably? Ask the Court to take judicial notice of the witness behaviour. While this may not affect the District Justice's determination of competency, or the strength of

---

[137] *Commonwealth v. Baker, 466 Pa. 479 (Pa. 1976), citing Commonwealth v. Ware, supra, 459 Pa. at 351-357, 329 A.2d at 267-69 (1974).* See also *Commonwealth v. Kosh, supra, 305 Pa. at 156, 157 A. at 482 (1931); Rosche v. McCoy, 397 Pa. 615, 620-21, 156 A.2d 307, 310 (1959); Dulnikowski v. Stanziano, 195 Pa.Super. 508, 510, 172 A.2d 182, 183 (1961).*

[138] *Commonwealth v. Delbridge, 578 Pa. at 664, 855 A.2d at 40.* See *Delbridge* for further reading regarding incompetency of child witnesses in sexual assault cases where taint or coercive methods of memory reconstruction have been employed.

[139] *United States v. Garner, 581 F.2d 481, 485 (5th Cir. 1978); United States v. Jackson, 576 F.2d 46, 48 (5th Cir. 1978).*

the Commonwealth's case, it may prove valuable to Counsel in seeking a pre-trial competency hearing or psychiatric evaluation before the Court of Common Pleas. See *Appendix 24* for a sample motion requesting a psychiatric examination based on a witness' behaviour at the time of the Preliminary Hearing.

§ 4-2   The Arrest

An arrest is defined as: "The taking of a person into custody for the purpose of bringing him before a court. The arresting person must have legal authority, must adequately communicate his intent to arrest, and must actually restrain the arrested person for the act to be called an arrest. He must have probable cause to seize and detain; i.e., suspicion is not enough."[140]

The only requirement for an "arrest" is some act by an officer indicating his intention to detain or take a person into custody and thereby subject that person to the actual control and will of the officer; no formal declaration of arrest is required.[141] The standard for determining whether police have initiated custodial interrogation or arrest is objective, with due consideration given to reasonable impression conveyed to person interrogated rather than strictly subjective view of the law enforcement officer or of the person being seized.[142]

PRACTICE TIP
Police Officers will often explicitly utter the word "arrest" when taking the Defendant into

---

[140] Gilbert Law Dictionary, 17, Harcourt Brace Legal and Professional Publications, Inc., New York, 1994
[141] *Commonwealth v. Brown, 326 A.2d 906 Pa.Super.,1974*
[142] *Commonwealth v. Edmiston, 634 A.2d 1078 Pa.,1993*

> custody. While Defense Counsel may be able to prove seizure of the person occurred prior thereto, it is certainly not likely that the arrest occurred at any time thereafter. Defense Counsel should therefore be certain to ask any testifying Police Officer when the first time the word "arrest" was uttered, and when the Defendant was first explicitly told he or she was under arrest.

The United States Supreme Court case of *Miranda v. Arizona, 384 U.S. 436 (U.S. 1966)* established that a person undergoing arrest or custodial interrogation must be warned of his or her right to remain silent, that anything he says can be used against him in court, that he has the right to consult with an attorney of his own choice and to have that attorney present while he answers any questions and that, if he is unable to afford an attorney, one will be provided for him before he is asked any questions.[143]

Sometimes the moment of arrest is clear. When a defendant is handcuffed and taken into custody, he or she is under arrest.[144] Police officers are professionals, and are often diligent in following procedure and reading the defendant *Miranda* and *O'Connell* warnings at the appropriate time. However, it can occasionally be unclear as to the moment when arrest occurs.[145] In those cases where statements are made to the police, or evidence is obtained, determining the time of arrest

---

[143] The decision in Miranda was then made applicable to all Pennsylvania cases by *Commonwealth v. Leaming 247 A.2d 590 Pa. 1968.*
[144] Commonwealth v. Roscioli, 361 A.2d 834 Pa.Super.,1976.
[145] See *Commonwealth v. Holmes, Mass., 183 N.E.2d 279, 280, 281 Mass. 1962*, which held that officers are not required to make any formal declaration of arrest or even to use the word "arrest."

can be of vital importance. Defendants frequently tell the police about their activities at the time of arrest or interrogation.[146]

Such statements are seldom made to the advantage of the defendant's case. For example, in a DUI case, if the defendant is truthful about the amount of alcohol consumed such statements often supply additional evidence for the Commonwealth; if the statements are part of an attempt to deceive the officer, they can be used to impugn the defendant's later statements, or even prevent him/her from taking the stand out of a fear of impeachment. It is therefore the task of the attorney to confirm when the arrest occurred, that the defendant received and understood his/her rights at the time of arrest, and any statements made in response to questions following arrest, but without *Miranda* warnings, are challenged in a pre-trial proceeding.[147]

§ 4-3   Corpus Delicti

"The Body of the Crime."[148]

---

[146] These statements are made for a variety of reasons. Although it may seem clear in hindsight that the defendant should have remained silent, and any statements seem the result of a colossal stupidity, remember that he/she is often under great pressure at the time of arrest; additionally, the defendant may be clinging to an image of the police officer as a friendly upholder of American values, the defendant may be pleading with the officer in an attempt to escape arrest, and/or the defendant may be intimidated by the officer's presence.

[147] See *Commonwealth v. Bonser, 258 A.2d 675 Pa.Super.,1969* for the proposition that the charge of an "indictable offense" falls within category of "criminal case" or "criminal prosecution" as those terms are used in Fifth and Sixth Amendments, and defendant charged with such an offense is entitled to *Miranda* warnings before being subjected to custodial interrogation.

[148] "The body of the crime. The body (material substance) upon which a crime has been committed, e.g. the corpse of a murdered man, the charred remains of a house burned down. In a derivative sense, the objective proof or substantial fact that a crime has been committed. The "corpus delicti" of a crime is the body, foundation or substance of the crime, which ordinarily includes two elements:

The Corpus Delicti rule provides that before introducing a Defendant's extra-judicial admission or confession, the Commonwealth must first establish that a crime has been committed by someone.[149] The rule is rooted in the hesitancy to convict a person of a crime solely on the basis of that person's statements.[150]

Note that the Commonwealth is not required to prove the existence of a crime beyond a reasonable doubt before the introduction of such statements. Rather, it is enough for the Commonwealth to prove that the injury or loss is more consistent with a crime having been committed than not.[151] Furthermore, the corpus delicti may be proven by circumstantial evidence. The prosecution's duty does not extend to affirmatively excluding the possibility of accident in order to establish the corpus delicti.[152]

To establish a criminal case, the Commonwealth has the burden of showing: a) that a loss or injury has occurred; b) that this loss occurred through a criminal agency, and c) that the accused was, in fact, the perpetrator of the deed.[153] The corpus delicti rule consists of the first two elements: the occurrence of a loss or injury, and some person's criminal conduct as the source of that loss or injury. The identity of the person responsible for the criminal act is not part of the corpus delicti.[154]

For illustrative purposes, see the case of *Commonwealth v. DeLeon 419 A.2d 82 Pa.Super.1980.* In that matter, a driving

---

the act and the criminal agency of the act." Black, Henry Campbell. Black's Law Dictionary, Sixth Edition. St. Paul Minn. West Publishing Co. 1991.

[149] *Commonwealth v. Sestina 546 A.2d 109 (Pa.Super.,1988)*

[150] *Id*

[151] *Commonwealth v. Zugay, 2000 PA Super 15 (Pa. Super. Ct. 2000)*

[152] *Commonwealth v. May 451 Pa. 31, 301 A.2d 368 (Pa.1973)*

[153] *Id*

[154] *Zugay*

under the influence case, the court ruled that the Commonwealth had proven the corpus delicti prior to the extra-judicial admission being admitted. There was evidence introduced that an automobile knocked down a stop sign and left considerable skid marks, as well as testimony of the police officer that the Defendant and apparent operator of the vehicle had the odour of alcohol on his breath. All this information is consistent with the fact that someone operated a motor vehicle while under the influence of intoxicating liquor, and so the Defendant's statements about drinking and being in control of the vehicle were admitted during the Commonwealth's case.

The corpus delicti rule is applicable at the time of the Preliminary Hearing.[155] Counsel should consider whether such an objection will serve his or her client, or if the objection is better reserved for trial.

PRACTICE TIP

The order of witnesses at the time of trial for the Commonwealth's case is subject to no formalized rule or procedural requirement. However, Counsel can often get a feel for the likely order of witnesses based on how they are presented at the Preliminary Hearing. If the Commonwealth calls the Police Officer before the alleged victim in a sexual assault case at the Preliminary Hearing, it is entirely possible the same order will be maintained at trial. Counsel

---

[155] *Commonwealth v. Meder, 611 A.2d 213, 216 (Pa. Super. Ct. 1992)* "The corpus delicti rule is a rule of evidence. *Commonwealth v. May, 451 Pa. 31, 301 A.2d 368 (1973). It* has been held that the law of evidence is often relaxed at a preliminary hearing. [citation omitted] The question here is whether the law of evidence is so relaxed at a preliminary hearing so as to allow the use of a confession without proof of the corpus delicti of the crime charged." *Meder at 6.*

should prepare for this possibility as well as the chances of mounting a successful Corpus Delicti challenge to the evidence at the time of trial.

If, as often happens, the investigating Police Officer testifies about Defendant's statement before the testimony of the victim or any evidence of a crime is introduced, then Counsel should seriously consider making the appropriate Corpus Delecti objection at that time. While aware Prosecution attorneys can recover from this objection by shifting the order of their witnesses, it may significantly throw them off balance, and open up additional avenues of attack for Defense Counsel.

A careful cross examination that is transcribed for use later, with particular attention paid to the timeline of events is the best reference in those cases where this rule will be relevant.

§ 4-4   Hearsay Evidence

Hearsay is defined in Pennsylvania as a statement, other than one made by the declarant while testifying at the trial or hearing, offered in evidence to prove the truth of the matter asserted.[156] A statement includes any oral or written assertion, and any nonverbal conduct if it is intended as an assertion.[157] The declarant is the person who makes the statement.[158]

---

[156] *PA.R.E. 801(c)*
[157] *PA.R.E. 801(a)*
[158] *PA.R.E. 801(b)*

Hearsay statements may not be introduced as evidence because they are viewed as inherently unreliable.[159]

The testimony of a witness as to what a third party told him about an alleged criminal act is clearly inadmissible hearsay,[160] and thus, does not constitute legally competent evidence. Hearsay evidence is not admissible at a Preliminary Hearing,[161] and standing alone hearsay evidence is insufficient to meet the burden of a prima facie case.[162]

There are several exceptions to hearsay that might apply. Some of these exceptions depend upon the declarant being unavailable[163] for cross-examination purposes,[164] some require the presence of the declarant,[165] and others have no such requirement.[166] Note that there may also be statutory exceptions to the hearsay rule elsewhere in Pennsylvania law.[167]

Proper objections to the Commonwealth's Case can sometimes make the difference between one that is bound over for trial, or dismissed at the time of the Preliminary Hearing. While Defense Counsel should thoroughly familiarize him or herself with these rules of evidence and be prepared for the

---

[159] *PA.R.E. 802*

[160] *Commonwealth v. Maybee, 429 Pa. 222, 239 A.2d 332 (1968), Commonwealth v. Whitner, 444 Pa. 556, 281 A.2d 870 (1971)*

[161] *Commonwealth v. Verbonitz. 525 Pa. 413, 581 A.2d 172 (1990),*

[162] *Commonwealth v. Camacho, 2007 Pa.D&C Chester County (Pa. County Ct. 2007)* citing *Commonwealth Ex Rel. Buchanan v. Verbonitz, 525 Pa. 413, 581 A.2d 172 (Pa. 1990), plurality decision; Commonwealth v. Jackson, 2004 PA Super 150, 849 A.2d 1254, 1257 (Pa. Super. 2004).*

[163] Death of the declarant is considered unavailability. *PA.R.E. 804(a)(4)*

[164] *PA.R.E. 804*

[165] *PA.R.E. Rule 803.1*

[166] *PA.R.E. Rule 803*

[167] See for example *42 Pa.C.S. § 5919,* which provides that in criminal matters a deposition of a witness may be read into evidence, or *42 Pa.C.S. § 5985.1,* which allows hearsay evidence as it relates to the testimony of child witnesses, or *42 Pa.C.S. § 5986* as it relates to the testimony of child victims.

opportunity to object, there may be other considerations that would restrain such an objection.

1.   If Defense Counsel is using the Preliminary Hearing as a method of gaining information, similar to a deposition, then objections to testimony as hearsay will only limit the width of the net that Counsel is able to cast. In such circumstances Defense Counsel's goal should be to gather as much information as possible, not to prohibit its introduction.

2.   If Defense Counsel intends to use the hearsay statements as a method to impeach the testimony of another witness. For example, at the time of the Preliminary Hearing, Police Officer A testifies that his fellow Officer B told him "the defendant had blood shot eyes". On examination of Officer B, he reveals that the defendant did not have blood shot eyes, but rather had blurry eyes. Defense Counsel can now use the hearsay statement of Officer B to A as a prior inconsistent statement at the time of trial.

This sort of impeachment would not be available if Defense Counsel had made an automatic objection to the testimony of Officer A. Counsel should remember that simply because evidence is admitted at a Preliminary Hearing does not mean it will automatically be admitted at trial.

§ 4-5   Jurisdictional Issues

Municipal Police Officers are granted the authority to arrest individuals outside of their jurisdiction only in certain cases:[168] Where the officer is in hot pursuit,[169] where the officer

---

[168] *42 Pa.C.S.A. § 8953*

is on official business approved by the Magisterial District Justice[170] or Chief Police Officer[171] of the jurisdiction, where the officer has been requested to aid, or has probable cause to believe that such aid is needed by, another officer,[172] where the officer is on official business and views an offense which presents clear and present danger to persons or property,[173] or when the officer views the commission of a felony.[174]

The Municipal Police Jurisdiction Act is not within the class of statutes that are to be strictly construed, but must be liberally construed to promote the interests of justice. The purpose of the Act is to provide a general limitation on extraterritorial patrols while allowing some exceptions for activity in response to specifically identified criminal behavior occurring within the primary jurisdiction of police.[175]

When a police officer acts under colour of state law outside his jurisdiction, his actions are deemed unlawful pursuant to the Municipal Police Jurisdiction Act. When a

---

[169] *42 Pa.C.S.A. § 8953(a)(2)* Police officers met hot and fresh pursuit standard of Municipal Police Jurisdiction Act (MPJA), and, therefore, were entitled to arrest defendant in neighboring township for driving under the influence of alcohol, where concerned citizens saw defendant hit two parked automobiles in officers' primary jurisdiction and instantaneously followed defendant in their own vehicles, citizens gave police information to identify defendant's vehicle and location where he fled, and, on this information, following only a very short interval after the accidents, police went to location where defendant had fled. *Commonwealth v. McPeak, 708 A.2d 1263, Super.1998.*

[170] *42 Pa.C.S.A. § 8953(a)(1)* If Police Officer strayed from his jurisdictional patrol and then noticed the Defendant, the officer was not on "official business." Police officer is not on "official business," within meaning of this section, allowing officer to enforce laws in another jurisdiction, any time officer, while on duty in his or her jurisdiction and enters another jurisdiction. *Commonwealth v. Merchant, 560 A.2d 795, 385 Pa.Super. 264, Super.1989.*

[171] *42 Pa.C.S.A. § 8953(a)(4)*

[172] *42 Pa.C.S.A. § 8953(a)(3)*

[173] *42 Pa.C.S.A. § 8953(a)(5)*

[174] *42 Pa.C.S.A. § 8953(a)(6)*

[175] *Commonwealth v. McGrady, 685 A.2d 1008, 454 Pa.Super. 444, Super.1996.*

police officer's actions are unlawful pursuant to the Municipal Police Jurisdiction Act, the exclusionary rule applies, and any evidence obtained as a result of the officer's actions must be suppressed[176].

PRACTICE TIP

Defense Counsel is not expected to be an expert on the jurisdictional regions of various municipal police departments, which often overlap or are unclear to the Officers themselves. Where the authority of a police officer to conduct a stop or arrest is in question based on the location of the incident, the client is best served by Counsel performing a vigorous and specific examination of the officer as to the places and times of the incidents in question.

For example, in a DUI prosecution, specifically ask about the location of first observation. Where was the Police Officer? "On Main Street" is not a sufficient answer. Require the Officer to specify where on Main Street the initial observation took place, using local businesses or landmarks as a guide. Follow up with the specific location of the Defendant at the time of the first observation. Then the specific location of the Officer at the time of the first suspicious activity, as well as the location of the Defendant at that time. Finally inquire as to the specific location where the vehicle stop took place.

---

[176] *Commonwealth v. Bradley, 724 A.2d 351, Super.1999.*

> If Officers from other jurisdictions assisted in the stop or arrest, inquire into how they were alerted to the hearing and where they encountered the Defendant. A stop initiated by one Officer in his or her own jurisdiction may be valid, but if a search is subsequently performed in another jurisdiction, the seized evidence may be the subject of a suppression motion.

§ 4-6   Identification

Identity is an essential element in a criminal case, and must be proven at trial beyond a reasonable doubt.[177] Accordingly, proof of this element as to a prima facie level must be shown at the time of the Preliminary Hearing.

Unfortunately at the time of the Preliminary Hearing, when the affiant comes face to face with a man or woman seated at Defendant's table and in handcuffs, it may be too late to attack identity issues. It is likely that the affiant will form a mental picture of Defendant and associate it with criminal behaviour regardless of the actual identity of Defendant.

If Defense Counsel believes that identity will be an issue prior to the Preliminary Hearing, there are several options available, as laid out in *Moore v. Ill., 434 U.S. 220 (U.S. 1977)*

1. Counsel can request that the hearing be postponed until a lineup could be arranged at which the victim would view petitioner in a less suggestive setting.[178]

---

[177] *Commonwealth v. Bird, 1943, 33 A.2d 531, 152 Pa.Super. 648.*
[178] *United States v. Ravich, 421 F. 2d 1196, 1202-1203(CA2), cert. denied, 400 U.S. 834 (1970); Mason v. United States, 134 U.S. App. D.C. 280, 283 n. 19, 414*

2. Short of that, counsel could have asked that the victim be excused from the courtroom while the charges were read and the evidence against petitioner was recited, and that petitioner be seated with other people in the audience when the victim attempted an identification[179].

3. Counsel might have sought to cross-examine the victim to test her identification before it hardened[180].

The Court in *Moore* went on to say, "Because it is in the prosecution's interest as well as the accused's that witnesses' identifications remain untainted, [citation omitted] we cannot assume that such requests would have been in vain. Such requests ordinarily are addressed to the sound discretion of the court, [citation omitted]".

PRACTICE TIP

Defense Counsel should have an honest conversation with client about the alleged incidents based on the information contained in the affidavit of probable cause. Does Defendant recognize the names of any eyewitnesses? Is it possible these witnesses saw Defendant at the time and place alleged, or is it possible they are mistaken? Are there any corroborating pieces of evidence, such as videotapes or photographs of

---

F. 2d 1176, 1179 n. 19 (1969). Also, see *Appendix 16* For a Sample Motion Requesting a Pre-Hearing Lineup

[179] *Allen v. Rhay, 431 F.2d 1160, 1165 (CA9 1970), cert. denied, 404 U.S. 834 (1971)*

[180] *Cf. Haberstroh v. Montanye, 493 F. 2d 483, 485 (CA2 1974); United States ex rel. Riffert v. Rundle, 464 F. 2d 1348, 1351 (CA3 1972), cert. denied sub nom. Riffert v. Johnson, 415 U.S. 927 (1974).*

the Defendant?　If there exists a reasonable question as to the identity of the Defendant then Counsel should prepare accordingly.

5

CROSS EXAMINATION

There are many different kinds of potential witnesses which may be called to testify at the time of the Preliminary Hearing, however, this field is generally much smaller than that of the full trial. It is unlikely, for example, to face witnesses who would testify as to the character of the Defendant, since the Commonwealth is only tasked with establishing proof to the prima facie level.

Of those kinds of witnesses that Defense Counsel will face, there are just as many strategies to employ during questioning. Which strategy to employ depends on Counsel's objective. In his excellent re-iteration of the Commandments of Cross-Examination, Timothy A. Pratt explains that Commandment two should be to know the objective.

> "Before initiating a cross-examination of any witness, the lawyer should clearly bear in mind those points he or she wishes to make with that witness. And then, he or she should write them down. These points also should be discussed with those who are assisting at trial. Effective cross-examination cannot be accomplished without a clear understanding of which points are critical to the case, and which ones can be extracted most appropriately from each witness."[181]

Is the goal to secure a dismissal? Then leading questions, with pointed objections to non-responsive answers should be employed. Is the goal to gather as much information as possible? Then asking open-ended questions which allow the

---

[181] Pratt, Timothy A., The Ten Commandments of Cross-Examination, http://www.thefederation.org/documents/Pratt-SP03.htm

witness to testify about as much as possible is the preferred method.

The use of a Court Reporter to transcribe the testimony cannot be stressed enough. Without a proper transcript, recourse for errors at the Preliminary Hearing will be difficult to obtain. Additionally, the use of testimony to impeach statements made later at trial will be impossible without an accurate transcript.

§ 5-1   Who is the Audience?

The cross-examination is likely to be the most lengthy and involved portion of the Preliminary Hearing. Defense Counsel should be aware that his or her performance is or will be observed by several different evaluators. Counsel should accordingly pay attention to how his or her performance would be perceived by these evaluators, and adjust strategy and methodology as appropriate.

§ 5-1.1 The Client

This is likely the first opportunity Defense Counsel will have to showcase his or her skills as an attorney for the client. The client expects Counsel to be competent, skilled, and knowledgeable. This is the chance to justify the faith and level of responsibility entrusted to him or her by the client. Is counsel pursuing the case with an appropriate level of interest? Are those questions which are of particular importance to the client being asked? If not, has Defense Counsel satisfactorily explained to the client why those questions are not appropriate at this time?

Counsel should also be aware that this initial performance might form the basis for the client's decision whether or not to continue with the representation through trial. A weak performance at the Preliminary Hearing may convince a client that Counsel cannot be counted on to defend him or her in front of a jury, and may end the representation before it can truly begin.

PRACTICE TIP

At the conclusion of cross-examination of any particular witness, Defense Counsel should turn to his or her client and inquire off the record if there are any additional questions that the client considers relevant to the hearing. Counsel should be sure to request permission from the Magisterial District Justice to consult with the client, and keep the conversation short.

This inquiry accomplishes two goals. First, it ensures that no potentially relevant questions have been omitted by Counsel. Second, it gives the client the feeling of being involved with the case and a feeling of trust and cooperation is fostered between the client and Counsel. Counsel should carefully consider whether the client's questions are irrelevant, repetitious, or likely to provoke the ire of the Court before putting such inquiries to the witness.

---

§ 5-1.2 The Magisterial District Justice

The Magisterial District Justice is evaluating Defense Counsel's performance, especially in those cases where a dismissal of all or some of the charges is being requested. Magisterial District Justice's sit through many Preliminary Hearings, often consisting of similar testimony, and it is Defense Counsel's job to point out how this case is different from the typical criminal matter such that it is deserving of a dismissal.

Magisterial District Justices are also entitled to the respect of all participants. It does not benefit Defense Counsel to grumble along with the Defendant about perceived bad decisions or incorrect legal analysis.

§ 5-1.3 The Judge of the Court of Common Pleas

It is entirely possible that based on the testimony elicited from cross-examination that Defense Counsel will file a motion in front of the Court of Common Pleas, for suppression, lack of probable cause, or other such issues. In those cases, the Preliminary Hearing transcript can often be used as an exhibit or introduced as evidence before the Court in support of the motion. A clear line of questioning in the transcript will significantly enhance Defense Counsel's chances in these matters.

To assist the Court of Common Pleas, Counsel should consider breaking the cross-examination up into sections related to relevant subjects and potential pre-trial issues. For example, in a DUI case, it would be appropriate to go through all the questions related to the Field Sobriety Tests in one continuous block. Then, should a pre-trial suppression motion be filed which rests on the Field Sobriety Testing procedures, Counsel can point to that particular block of testimony to assist the Court in making its determination.

Of course, there are times when it is proper to jump around in subject matter so as to keep the witness off guard. The presentation of the transcript for the Court of Common Pleas must therefore be balanced with all other effective cross-examination methodology.

§ 5-1.4 Trial Jury

Should the case proceed to trial, inconsistent statements and/or the ability to quickly refresh the recollection of a witness may prove vital. Defense Counsel should consider how a particular line of questioning will play to a jury should it be necessary to have some of the transcript recited at that time.

Note that at trial it is often more effective to have the statement made by the witness, rather than a binary response to a question from Defense Counsel. For example, consider a retail theft case where at the time of the Preliminary Hearing the store's Loss Prevention Manager testified that Defendant was never in the store before the day in question. Then at trial, the Manager testifies that the Defendant had been in the store dozens of times in the past.

Review each of the following possible lines of question from the Preliminary Hearing. Which would play better when read to a jury, and be of stronger support for a contention that the Manager is either confused, or intentionally being deceptive?

Option 1:

Defense Counsel:
Isn't it true that the Defendant had never been in the store before the day in question?

Witness: Yes.

Option 2:

> <u>Defense Counsel:</u>
> What was the relationship between the Defendant and the store in question?
>
> <u>Witness:</u>
> There was no relationship.
>
> <u>Defense Counsel:</u>
> How many times had you seen her in the store before the day of the incident?
>
> <u>Witness:</u>
> **I've never seen her in the store before.**

While it may be more difficult to elicit the desired statement, the payoff of being able to directly contradict the witness' testimony with a directly quoted statement at the time of trial can be invaluable. Witnesses can later claim to have misunderstood the question of Defense Counsel, or can claim to have mistakenly answered the wrong inquiry. This becomes much more complicated to escape when the statement is coming directly from the Witness' prior testimony.

§ 5-1.5 Defense Counsel

Of concern should the case proceed past the Preliminary Hearing is the ability of Defense Counsel to quickly and effectively review the transcript for potential legal issues or inconsistent statements for trial. This is made all the more difficult by a disorganized cross-examination. Counsel should keep in mind that in prepping for trial he or she will be reviewing the transcript with a close eye. Anything that can be done in preparation for that contingency will pay off in saved time later. Additionally, should the case be transferred or surrendered to alternate counsel prior to trial, a carefully organized and constructed cross-examination can be reviewed by incoming counsel and important legal issues can be spotted well in advance.

§ 5-1.6 The Community and Potential Clients

Defense Counsel should also consider his or her performance as it relates to the public perception of the legal community. A poor performance which indicates Counsel is incompetent or unprepared casts doubt and shame on all Defense Attorneys, and does not hold the legal profession up to the rigorous standards required by the Rules of Professional Conduct.[182]

Private Defense Counsel should also be aware that observers, neutral third party witnesses, and others might serve as potential referrals for additional business. An attorney who competently and professionally represents his or her client at the time of the Preliminary Hearing will be remembered more fondly than one who fumbles throughout the hearing, is unprepared, or makes significant mistakes of procedure and law.

---

[182] See for example, *Rule of Professional Conduct 1.1*, Competence, which provides that "A lawyer shall provide competent representation to a client." Competent representation requires the legal knowledge, skill thoroughness and preparation reasonably necessary for representation."

Presented for Defense Counsel in the following section is a general guide to the basic, minimalist sorts of questioning which should be employed to secure information, while also allowing the opportunity to make strong legal arguments before the District Justice or a Court of Common Pleas based on the testimony presented. Defense Counsel should feel free to omit portions which are irrelevant to the case at hand, to add substantively to the guide, and to rearrange as necessary. There is no order of questioning which need be engaged, and it is often to Counsel's advantage to move around both chronologically and subjectively when facing resistance from a witness.

Among the kinds of witnesses, there are those who have observed some conduct committed by the Defendant. These witnesses should be thoroughly cross-examined with an eye to gaining specific information which can be correlated with the testimony of others, examined in light of any physical evidence, or used for possible impeachment.

§ 5-2 Observational witness

Ask the following questions about any observed behaviour, and try to get as specific answers as possible.

1.   When did the behaviour occur?

2.   Where did it occur?

3.   Where was the witness in relation to the incident?

      a. Was there any obstruction which might have interfered with the witness' observation?

4.   How long did the observation last?

a. Was the observation uninterrupted?

5. Who else was present at the time of the observation?

Often, testimony is presented regarding inculpatory statements made by the Defendant. In such cases, Defense Counsel should examine the circumstances surrounding the statements carefully.

1. Did the Defendant make any statements?

2. Who else overheard the statements?

3. What was Defendant's demeanour when statements made?

4. Where were the statements made? House, police station, side of road, inside vehicle, etc.

5. Where the statements made while Defendant was in custody?

6. Prior to or after being given Miranda warnings?

7. What were the exact questions which prompted Defendant's statement?

8. What was the exact answer given by the Defendant?

9. Were there any audio or video recordings of the statement made?

10. Any contemporaneous written notes taken at the time of the statement?

11.   How much time has passed since the statements were made?

12.   Was there any reason to disbelieve the statements?

§ 5-3   Civilian

The civilian witness is often presented by the Commonwealth as either an eyewitness to certain behaviour, or as victim of the alleged criminal activity. In either case, Defense Counsel should determine as soon as practicable what kind of testimony will be presented, and to structure the cross-examination accordingly.

With regard to the questioning, first determine whether the witness' competency to testify will be at issue. Then, with as wide a net as possible, inquire as to background of the witness to expose any additional defects or flaws in the testimony.

1.   What is witness' past relationship with Defendant?

   a.   If no prior relationship, how is witness able to confidently identify the Defendant?

2.   How did witness come to observe the Defendant's behaviour or actions?

3.   Was witness in a position where he or she could clearly observe the incident in question?

4.   Is witness' ability to accurately observe the incident in question?

   a.   Drug or alcohol use at the time of incident?

      b. Mental illness?

  5. Is witness' ability to testify truthfully impaired?

      a. Drug or alcohol use at the time of the Preliminary Hearing.

      b. Currently suffer from a mental illness?

      c. What is witness' criminal history, specifically any crimen falsi charges?

      d. Has witness been made any promises in exchange for his or her testimony?

      e. Does the witness suffer from any sort of bias or prejudice regarding the Defendant or any other participant or witness?

§ 5-4 Police Officer

The preliminary hearing is the first opportunity of defense counsel to cross examine the police officer and to asses the officer's testimony regarding the case investigation. It is important for defense counsel to be able to establish issues regarding probable cause to stop or arrest, as well as any other legal issues which may become relevant at a later time. Remember that Police Officers make very persuasive witnesses at trial, so laying the groundwork for a successful trial cross-examination should be paramount in any strategy. Defense counsel must thoroughly examine the police officer regarding everything the police officer observed from the time:

  1. that the police officer initially observed the defendant,

2. To the time the first suspicions of criminal behaviour surfaced,

3. As well as the initial encounter between the police officer and the Defendant,

4. Everything observed through investigation and questioning, including any possible field sobriety testing, interrogations, or the conditions as to whether the Defendant was free to leave, as well as,

5. The Defendant's actions after the arrest, and finally through

6. Processing.

Defense counsel will most likely encounter resistance from the police officer and possibly from the District Justice when cross-examining the police officer regarding the defendant's actions, but counsel should continue to vigorously cross-examine the police officer because he is often the prosecution's main witness.

All of the issues which are testified to on direct examination are relevant during cross-examination. If the District Justice attempts to eliminate cross-examination of the police officer on the basis that this is only a preliminary hearing and not a trial, defense counsel should strongly argue that all the matters were testified to on direct examination and defense counsel has the opportunity and the right to cross examine as to those incidents which were testified to on direct. Defense counsel should not be intimidated into not cross-examining the police officer.

CROSS-EXAMINATION

Additional question applicable to cross-examination of a police officer or law enforcement official include the following:

1. Prior experience in law enforcement.

    a. Both generally, and as it relates to the specific charges in question.

    b. Number of arrests and prosecutions for this type of crime.

2. Education.

    a. Has the officer received any specialized training with regard to this type of crime?

3. If incident and investigation was confined to a single night (i.e. as part of a vehicle stop) then inquire as to the Officer's tour of duty that night.

    a. Who else was on duty with officer?

    b. Who was responsible for filing reports with headquarters?

    c. Who else observed the incident or participated in the investigation?

    d. Who made the decision to stop and/or arrest the Defendant?

    e. What other kinds of incidents occurred during Officer's tour?

4. Investigation conducted:

a. Did the Officer conduct field sobriety tests, or any other kind of investigatory actions in the field?

b. Which tests were conducted?

c. What were the conditions of the testing?

d. For example, if a DUI suspect completed the one leg stand test, was the test conducted on level ground? Did the Officer demonstrate the test for the Defendant? How long did the demonstration last? Were the Emergency lights on the patrol car flashing while the test was conducted?

e. What were the specific articuable indications which the Officer observed which lead him to believe suspicious activity was afoot?

f. For example, if a motor vehicle stop leads the Officer to believe that drugs are present in the car, inquire as to the specifics which lead him or her to that conclusion. Were the Defendant's eyes glazed, blurry, red, or bloodshot? Was there an odour of an illicit substance in the car? Was the odour on the Defendant's breath, his clothing, the interior of the car, or emanating from somewhere else?

g. If incriminating evidence is discovered, delve into the specifics of the discovery.

h. For example, if an Officer is examining the interior of a Defendant's residence searching for illegal firearms and some are found then ask where the firearms were found? Were the firearms in a bag or container? Where was the bag? Was the bag fingerprinted or otherwise processed? Were the Defendant's fingerprints found on the bag or container?

PRACTICE TIP

Anytime illegal contraband is recovered, Defense Counsel should thoroughly examine the Officer as to the presence of fingerprints or DNA evidence found on or near the item. For example, if a bag containing illegal weapons is discovered, ask if fingerprints were found on the bag, or on any of the surfaces around where the bag was found. If a shooting occurred and shell casings are recovered, then inquire if fingerprints were found on the shell casings. If cigarette butts are visible in photographs near the scene, inquire if those cigarette butts were taken in for DNA processing.

In many cases, the likely answer is that these items were never processed. Securing that testimony at the time of the Preliminary Hearing can allow Counsel to develop an argument of insufficient police work at the time of trial.

---

5. The Arrest

a. Who else was present at the time of arrest?

b. Was there a lawful warrant issued for the arrest?

c. Was all information made available to the signatory on the warrant application?

d. If no warrant, what were the circumstances that justified a warrantless arrest?

e. Where did the arrest take place?

f. Why was that location chosen?

g. Was any incriminating evidence discovered during the arrest process?

h. How many officers made the actual arrest?

i. Was Defendant put into handcuffs? If so, when and by whom?

j. What statements were made TO the Defendant at the time of arrest? (Miranda warnings, etc).

k. Who made those statements?

l. Were those statements read , recited from memory or presented in written form for Defendant?

m. Did anyone actually use the word "arrest"?

n. Who, when and in what context?

o. When was the first time the word arrest was actually spoken aloud?

      p. Did anyone suggest to Defendant that he might be arrested prior to actually being placed in handcuffs?

6. Statements

      a. Did Defendant make any statements at arrest? If so, who else witnessed these statements?

      b. Was Defendant advised of his or her right to remain silent?

      c. Did he exercise that right?

      d. Was he in a condition to do so? (Injured, intoxicated, etc.).

      e. What were the conditions under which Defendant made the statement? How long had he been in custody? Was he denied access to an attorney, a Doctor, or the opportunity to speak with a family member?

7. Witness statements

      a. Were there any statements from other parties the Officer relied on in making his or her decision to arrest the Defendant?

      b. Were those statements audio or video recorded?

      c. Were they written or oral statements?

      d. Were those statements consistent with the other findings of the Officer's investigation?

e.   Were the statements consistent with each other?

f.   Were the statements internally consistent?

§ 5-5   Expert Witness

Facing down an expert witness secured by the Commonwealth can be an intimidating prospect for Defense Counsel, especially if the expert is one who has experience testifying. Whether it is a medical professional testifying about the results of a "rape kit" exam, or a trained officer testifying about the process of obtaining blood alcohol concentration results, Defense Counsel should proceed by properly preparing for the cross-examination.

Thoroughly cross-examine the expert both about his or her qualifications and as to the actual work conducted related to the matter. Many experts will simply have reviewed the work of others, and may have no first hand knowledge of the specific facts of the case. Remember that witnesses may only testify as an expert pursuant to the Rules of Evidence[183]. The standard for qualification of an expert witness is "whether the witness has any reasonable pretension to specialized knowledge on the subject under investigation[184]." Additionally, the testimony offered must have general acceptance in the relevant scientific

---

[183] *Pa.R.E. 702.* Testimony by experts "If scientific, technical or other specialized knowledge beyond that possessed by a layperson will assist the trier of fact to understand the evidence or to determine a fact in issue, a witness qualified as an expert by knowledge, skill, experience, training or education may testify thereto in the form of an opinion or otherwise."

[184] *Miller v. Brass Rail Tavern, 541 Pa. 474, 664 A.2d 525, 528 (Pa. 1995)*

community[185].   Defense Counsel therefore has every right to
cross examine the qualifications and the breadth of actual review
or work done on the case.

1.   Background.

    a. Education

    b. Specific education related to issues at hand (BAC
        training, Human physiology, psychology, etc...)

    c. How long has the expert worked at his or her current
        position?

    d. What kind of specialized knowledge has he or she
        gained into these types of cases?

    e. How many times has he or she done this same kind of
        examination/review? (For example, how many blood
        samples for BAC purposes has the person taken
        without assistance or guidance from a superior? How
        many rape kits has the person completed on his or her
        own? How many psychological assessments of
        similar patients has the expert completed? How many
        times has the expert used that particular Intoxilyzer
        BAC analyzer machine in the past?)

    f. Most recent training or education on this topic.

    g. How many times has the expert testified in these
        kinds of matters?

---

[185] *A.J.B. v. M.P.B., 2008 PA Super 39, P13 (Pa. Super. Ct. 2008) citing Grady, 839 A.2d at 1046; Commonwealth v. Arroyo, 555 Pa. 125, 723 A.2d 162, 170 (Pa. 1999).*

h. How many times for the Commonwealth? Ever for Defendant?

i. How much compensation is the expert receiving for his or her testimony?

2. Work on the instant case

a. When did the expert become familiar with the facts of the case?

i. Who related those facts to the expert?

ii. Was it a written statement or an interview?

b. Did expert ever interview or observe the Defendant?

i. What kind of specific observations were made?

ii. Was interview audio or video recorded?

iii. How long did interview or observation last?

iv. Did expert follow all applicable procedures required during interview or examination? For example, did the expert follow all required instructions for use of the BAC test device? Did the expert provide the proper instructions to Defendant before administering the test?

c. Did the expert interview or observe a third party?

i. What kind of specific observations were made?

ii. Was expert given any background on the case prior to the examination or interview?

iii. How long did it last? Any follow up exams or interviews?

iv. Has the expert ever treated or interviewed the person previously?

v. Did the expert review any relevant medical, psychological or personal history prior to the exam or interview?

vi. Which portions of the exam or interview were actually conducted by those under the expert's auspice, and which portions were actually done by the expert him or herself? For example, did the expert personally complete the DNA swabs for the rape kit? Did the expert personally analyze the blood sample to determine the BAC level?

3. Expert's conclusions

a. What other information did the expert base his or her opinion on that hasn't been presented yet at court?

b. Is the opinion presented by the expert to a reasonable degree of certainty?

PRACTICE TIP

Most expert witnesses retained by the Commonwealth have been extensively trained in how to answer questions so as to add support to the Prosecution's case, while admitting little

---

possibility for doubt. While Defense Counsel should always consider whether an opposing expert is necessary for trial, significant groundwork in impeaching the credibility or impartiality of the Commonwealth's expert can be laid at the time of the Preliminary Hearing. A careful dissection of the expert's methodology and basis for conclusions made will be particularly helpful.

c. If a machine or tool was used in the procedure or exam, when was the last time that machine or tool was calibrated?

d. Who is responsible for calibrating the machine or tool?

e. Is the opinion the kind that would be generally accepted by others in the medical field?

While it is unlikely the expert would admit his or her opinion is not generally accepted, this provides a good follow up in the form of "Could there be any other possible explanation for the evidence you reviewed other than the conclusion you have presented?" For example, is it possible the person's BAC level was lower, but the machine malfunctioned and had a higher reading? The expert will answer this one of two ways. He or she may admit it is possible the machine could have malfunctioned, which can be of great value later at trial. Alternatively, the expert will make an absolutist statement which can be easily turned against his or her credibility at trial, or Defense Counsel can produce his or her own expert to discredit such an absolutist statement.

This sort of attack can be especially potent if Defense Counsel can secure the records of the expert or the machine for the recent past. Examine same to determine if any erroneous results have ever appeared. It is not uncommon for BAC machines to undergo periodic calibration adjustments, requiring them to be taken out of service. When the expert is cross-examined at the time of trial, and he or she still adheres to the absolutist position held at the preliminary hearing, the use of those records can be devastating.

§ 5-6   Final Notes on Cross-Examination

The Cross-examination of Commonwealth witnesses is a devastating weapon in Defense Counsel's arsenal. The ability to ask a wide range of questions, develop legal issues, and prepare for trial is immensely useful for trial preparation. Competent Defense Counsel will adequately prepare for this opportunity and use it to the full extent allowed by the rules of procedure and the patience of the Magisterial District Justice.

PRACTICE TIP

There is one caveat to the use of Preliminary Hearings as a discovery device – if Counsel believes a legal challenge is imminent and likely to succeed, then he or she may wish to hold back on extended questioning in the hopes that the failure of the Commonwealth to fully develop the testimony is fatal to the prosecution. For example, consider a DUI case, in which no statement is made regarding the BAC testing device. No citation is made to the applicable PA

Bulletin and no documents establishing the BAC level of Defendant are introduced in evidence.

Normally, Defense Counsel should examine the affiant to discover as much information as possible about the machine in question, including the model number, in service dates, and operator's certification. However, if the Commonwealth ends their direct examination without introducing the appropriate evidence, Defense Counsel may wish to forego this normal range of questioning in order to make the legal argument at closing that the Commonwealth failed to meet their burden by not introducing this information during their presentation.

6

PRESENTATION OF THE
DEFENDANT'S CASE

§ 6-1   Defendant's Testimony

At the Conclusion of the Commonwealth's Case, the Defendant is entitled to testify and present any evidence he or she feels would successfully rebut the Commonwealth's case. As iterated elsewhere in this guide, it is not usually in the Defendant's best interests to testify or present any witnesses. However, convincing one's client that this is the case can be a difficult task.

Defense Counsel should make sure that the client fully understands the burden of proof required at the Preliminary Hearing. Most adult Americans have heard the expression "beyond a reasonable doubt" through their exposure to television courtroom justice. Few have heard of "prima facie" or have any idea what it means or how it applies to their case.

Defense Counsel should explain that the Magisterial District Justice is required by law to bind the case over for trial if it appears that a crime has been committed, and that the Defendant has some connection with that crime. He or she is not being found guilty or innocent – and that should be stressed. The Preliminary Hearing is only one step in the long process that is the Pennsylvania Criminal Justice System.

With that out of the way, Defense Counsel should consider calling the Defendant to testify or present witnesses in those cases where such testimony can easily rebut allegations or assumptions made by the Commonwealth in the presentation of their case.

PRACTICE TIP

Counsel may face a difficult time convincing his or her client that it is not good strategy to testify on one's own behalf at the time

---

of the Preliminary Hearing. There can be a strong emotional pull on the Defendant to want to have his or her story heard.

While Defense Counsel must balance the Defendant's desire with a realistic view of the Commonwealth's case, Counsel must remember that it is ultimately the client whose freedom is at issue. In those circumstances where the client decides to testify or otherwise ignore advice, Counsel must continue to work toward a just resolution of the matter.

Counsel concerned with the truthfulness of a Defendant's testimony should consult the Rules of Professional Conduct with regard to presenting testimony believed to be false. Specifically, see Rules of Professional Conduct 1.2 and 4.1.

However, allowing the Defendant to testify at the Preliminary Hearing can also have negative consequences. The successful use of Defendant's testimony at a Preliminary Hearing is rare, and should be exercised with the greatest degree of caution. Unless Defense Counsel encounters a similar situation where the Defendant's testimony can clear up this kind of issue, it is better practice not to present such testimony.

Presenting the Defendant's testimony carries with it the following possible negative outcomes:

1. It alerts the Commonwealth as to the potential defenses to be used by Defendant at the time of trial. The element of surprise is not afforded to the Commonwealth at trial. The Discovery rules prohibit the introduction of evidence not

previously disclosed to the Defendant. This does not necessarily work in reverse, and except for those specific enumerated types of evidence which Defense Counsel must disclose to the Prosecution, the substance of Defendant's case may remain protected. If the Defendant does testify at the Preliminary Hearing, then the Commonwealth can then prepare its own case to attack these defenses at trial before the Defense ever has an opportunity to present them.

2.   It locks the Defendant into statements before he has had a chance to go over his version of events with Counsel. It is rare that Defense Counsel is hired well in advance of the Preliminary Hearing, and preparation with the client may amount to a few isolated meetings and a discussion of the procedure. Defense Counsel will often have only the Affidavit of Probable Cause on which to base his or her assumptions about the Commonwealth's case. In this environment, to have the Defendant testify would be to put him or her in a situation without adequate preparation or warning, which could potentially lock Defendant into a version of events which has not been reviewed by Defense Counsel for accuracy or relation with other facts. The transcript of this testimony will most assuredly be used against the Defendant at the time of trial just as Defense Counsel would use the transcript against the Commonwealth's witnesses.

Contrast this with the possible benefits of Defendant's testimony. Even if Defendant testifies and is believable, it is unlikely to result in a dismissal, as credibility is not an issue for the Preliminary Hearing. Defense Counsel should explain to his or her client that even if the Magisterial District Justice believes the Defendant and disbelieves the affiant, the charges must be bound over for Court as only a jury can make such determinations about the truthfulness of a witnesses' testimony.

§ 6-2   Presenting Witnesses

Similar reasoning underscores the decision not to present the testimony of third party witnesses. The same negative consequences of alerting the Commonwealth, and locking witnesses into unknown testimony are just as present with these potential witnesses as it is with the Defendant himself.

There are some other exceptions to this general rule however, which would not apply in the case of the Defendant testifying. In the following limited circumstances Defense Counsel may wish to consider calling a third aprty witness to testify.

1.   The witness has a potential likelihood of not appearing later at the time of trial. Defense Counsel should consider the reliability of the third party involved to appear at trial. Is the witness aged or infirmed? Is it a strong possibility he or she will be deceased by the time the case gets in front of a jury? Is the witness liable to flee the jurisdiction before trial? Is the witness notoriously hard to contact, and unlikely to surface again for the trial? In such cases Defense Counsel should secure the testimony at the Preliminary Hearing to ensure it is available in some form at the time of trial.

If the answer to any of these questions is yes, then Defense Counsel should seriously consider calling the third party witness to testify at the time of the Preliminary Hearing to ensure important testimony is not lost due to the unavailability of the witness.

2.   The witness has the potential to change his or her testimony before the time of trial. Is the Defendant engaged in a personal relationship with the third party which may sour in the intervening months and put him or her at odds with the current testimony? Does the third party face criminal charges of his or her own which would make willing testimony at a later date unlikely?

Once again, if Defense Counsel believes that this circumstance applies then it may be in the client's best interests to preserve the testimony as it now exists.

§ 6-3   Introducing Evidence

While not as potentially destructive to the Defendant's case, it may still be wise for Defense Counsel to withhold the display or production of evidence at the Preliminary Hearing. Pictures, audio or video recordings, or other items which have an effect on the credibility of witnesses are unlikely to influence the decision of the Magisterial District Justice, and will only serve to alert the Commonwealth to their existence, and allow them to better prepare for their introduction at trial.

There are some circumstances however where introducing evidence is advised.

1.   The evidence is being introduced not for their probative value but for the effect that the evidence will have on the witness. Evidence that is at odds with the testimony of a Commonwealth witness may be introduced at the time of the Preliminary Hearing simply to discover what kind of effect it will have on the witness. This prepares Defense Counsel for what the explanation will be at trial, and allows for more strategic use at that time.

For example, a photograph showing facts contrary to the witness' testimony could be introduced, and the witness then asked to explain the discrepancy. Whatever explanation given by the witness, if one is even provided, will then be expected at trial and Defense Counsel will not be asking a question he or she doesn't know the answer to.

PRACTICE TIP

It is entirely possible a witness has a completely reasonable explanation for the contradictory evidence that Defense Counsel simply hasn't considered. It is better to know that ahead of time then face embarrassment and potential loss of credibility with a jury at the time of trial.

While it is possible for the witness to have no explanation at the Preliminary Hearing, but to conveniently come up with something at the time of trial, this can be easily attacked and is more often to backfire on the witness as long as Defense Counsel has a copy of the transcript.

---

2.   The evidence is being introduced to ensure recognition, refresh recollection or some other procedural purpose which will make the introduction of the evidence easier at the time of trial. At trial, Defense Counsel should be thoroughly prepared to fight for the introduction of all evidence over the potential objections of the Commonwealth. If a photograph has been pre-identified, or an audio recording testified to as accurate at the Preliminary hearing, it makes introduction at trial much easier.

Counsel should seriously consider whether the above rationale, or some other relevant reasoning applies before attempting to introduce evidence at the time of the Preliminary hearing. Evidence that merely attempts to attack the credibility of Commonwealth's witnesses is unlikely to have an effect on the outcome of the case, so unless there are other considerations the Defendant's best interests may be better served by reserving the evidence for trial.

§ 6-4 Closing Argument

Unlike the possible negative consequences attendant to Defendant's testimony, Defense Counsel's closing argument suffers from no such defects. Contrary to the pitfalls attendant a Defendant's testimony, Defense Counsel's closing argument suffers from no such defects. A well-made closing argument serves several purposes.

1.   The closing argument distills the objections to the Commonwealth's case into a short summary that the Magisterial District Justice can use to consider rejecting the case.

2.   It establishes for the client that Defense Counsel is competently pursuing his or her best interests, and is making a strong case despite the allegations of the Commonwealth.

PRACTICE TIP

Defendants naturally seek approval of their attorneys in the hope that someone believes they are not guilty of the charges. Being accused of a crime, especially falsely or where the

---

charges have been inflated, is a frustrating experience for the criminal defendant. For them to seek approval is natural, and they are more likely to be satisfied with Defense Counsel who expresses some belief in their story. While Defense Counsel should withhold final judgment and not become personally invested in the outcome of Defendant's case, Counsel should still make it clear to the Defendant that his or her case is important, and that Counsel is prepared to represent him or her to the best of Counsel's ability.

Procedurally, Defense Counsel should ask permission to address the Court, then rise at the table (to signify some statement of importance is about to be made) and then address the issues presented by the evidence and the Commonwealth's allegations. Counsel may approach the argument in any order he or she sees fit, but to organize it for the Magisterial District Justice the following schedule may be considered.

1. Chronological discussion of the witnesses testimony, including any lapses in testimony or internal contradictions.

2. A discussion of the legal issues raised, including whether or not the evidence presented rises to the level required for the finding of a prima facie level. Counsel would be wise to cite to the criminal statute specifically, and to indicate which required element is unsupported by the Commonwealth's case.

3.   A final portion setting forth the specific relief requested. While this may often be a dismissal of all charges, it may occasionally be more pointed such as a request for a dismissal of only certain charges which are unsupported by the evidence.

PRACTICE TIP

Do not make bail arguments in the Closing portion of the case. This presumes that the case will be bound over, and may weaken Defense Counsel's legal arguments for dismissal if the Magisterial District Justice is considering those bail arguments instead of whether or not to bind the charges over. It is only appropriate to modify bail at the conclusion of the case, and after the Magisterial District Justice has bound the charges over. If Counsel is in doubt as to whether the Magisterial District Justice will hear bail argument after the case has been presented, then a simple request at the conclusion of the Closing Argument to hold the record open for bail reconsideration should be sufficient. For example:

"...Accordingly your Honour, the Defense requests that all charges be dismissed for failure of the Commonwealth to establish a prima facie case. However, should this Court determine that sufficient evidence has been presented then I would request the opportunity to be heard on a bail modification after a decision is rendered."

> This preserves Defense Counsel's right to make a request for bail modification without sacrificing the strength of the legal arguments already presented.

§ 6-5 Samples of Closing Argument

Defense Counsel should consider tailoring his or her closing argument to the strongest or most important part of the Defendant's case. Focusing in on a few salient points is a good policy for beginning Counsel. Provided below are several example closings related to various charges. While each follows a similar format, they each attack a different part of the case. Defense Counsel is encouraged to adapt these arguments to the particular situation of his or her client, and to experiment with any other alternatives. This is by no means an exhaustive list of all potential avenues of attack, but provides a solid base for beginning Counsel.

1.   Attack the sufficiency of the evidence.

Consider a case where the Defendant has been charged with Conspiracy to commit Robbery.[186] The testimony consisted

---

[186] For the relevant criminal code as to Robbery see *18 Pa.C.S. § 3701(a)(1)* "a person is guilty of robbery if, in the course of committing a theft, he: (i) inflicts serious bodily injury upon another; [or] (ii) threatens another with or intentionally puts him in fear of immediate serious bodily injury." With regard to Criminal Conspiracy, see *18 Pa.C.S. § 903(a)* which provides that a "person is guilty of conspiracy with another person or persons to commit a crime if with the intent of promoting or facilitating its commission he: (1) agrees with such other person or persons that they or one or more of them will engage in conduct which constitutes such crime or an attempt or solicitation to commit such crime; or (2) agrees to aid such other person or persons in the planning or commission of such crime or of an attempt or solicitation to commit such crime." Also note section

of a storeowner and eyewitness who were robbed at gunpoint by a third person. Police then apprehended the robber within a few minutes riding in a pickup truck a few miles from the scene. The Defendant was driving the truck at the time and professed to have no connection with the robbery, only telling police he was driving his friend home. The Defendant was never identified as being involved by the storeowner and other than his presence in the vehicle had no connection with the incident.

Defense Counsel should consider attacking the sufficiency of the evidence offered by the Commonwealth. An example of such a closing might be as follows.

> "Your Honour, at this time the Defense would ask this Court to dismiss the Conspiracy charge against the Defendant. The commonwealth presented eyewitness testimony of a third party's guilt, and admittedly that evidence is strong as to that third party. However, there is a complete lack of evidence indicating my client's complicity in that event.

> There has been no evidence of a meeting of the minds or agreement between the third party and my client. No evidence of any step taken by the Defendant in furtherance of that plan. And no evidence that my client was even aware of what had happened inside the store on the day in question.

(e), which requires that "No person may be convicted of conspiracy to commit a crime unless an overt act in pursuant of such conspiracy is alleged and proved to have been done by him or by a person with whom he conspired."

As he said to the Officer, he was simply giving a friend a ride home and there has been nothing presented by the Commonwealth to support their case, certainly nothing rising to the level of prima facie. All they have is his friendship with the alleged robber. That's an attempt at guilt by association, your Honour, and this Court should not condone the arrest and prosecution of an individual based solely on his friends and acquaintances.

While the prima facie level of evidence is a low burden for the Commonwealth to reach, they still must show something to support the charges. As they have failed to introduce anything to support their accusations, the charges must be dismissed."

2.   **Attack one particular element of the crime charged.**

In this case, the client is charged with corruption of a minor.[187] The Commonwealth has introduced evidence that the client conspired with her daughter to engage in retail theft in the form of eyewitness testimony. This eyewitness testified that the Defendant and her daughter worked together to take various items from a retail store and leave without tendering payment. However, the Commonwealth introduced no affirmative

---

[187] *18 Pa.C.S. § 6301(a)(1)* "Whoever, being of the age of 18 years and upwards, by any act corrupts or tends to corrupt the morals of any minor less than 18 years of age, or who aids, abets, entices or encourages any such minor in the commission of any crime, or who knowingly assists or encourages such minor in violating his or her parole or any order of court, commits a misdemeanor of the first degree."

evidence that the daughter was under the age of 18. An excellent tactic in this case is to attack the sufficiency of the evidence as it relates to the daughter's "minor status".

"Your Honour, at this time the Defense would ask for a dismissal of the corruption of minors charge. The Commonwealth introduced evidence here today that the Defendant conspired with another person to engage in the crime of retail theft, and we will acknowledge they have met their burden in that regard. However, they have failed to provide any affirmative evidence to the Court establishing the age of the Defendant's daughter. So we do not know she is a minor. We don't have a driver's license, a birth certificate, or even a statement by the daughter or her mother that she is below the age of majority.

Without evidence as to her age they cannot establish that she is a minor and therefore there is not a prima facie level of evidence to support that element of the crime charged. If the Commonwealth is unable to support every element of the crime charged at least to a prima facie level then the charge must be dismissed.

Accordingly your Honour, the Defense would request that the charge of corruption of a minor be dismissed. Thank you."

3. Attack one specific charge out of several.

In this case, the Defendant is charged with DUI,[188] as well as simple assault.[189] The evidence consists of the police officer's observations that he approached the scene of an automobile accident where the Defendant was in the driver's seat. The Defendant admitted to drinking, consented to a BAC test and blew a .15, well above the legal limit. During processing, the Defendant became combative with a second Officer and attacked him. The arresting officer did not observe the assault, and his attempts to testify about the hearsay testimony of the second officer were properly objected to and sustained by the District Justice.

A successful tactic in this case might be to point out that although the Commonwealth has provided ample evidence to support a prima facie case as to the DUI charge, they have failed introduce any competent evidence to sustain their burden on the assault charge.

> "Your Honour, at this time we would ask for a dismissal of the charge of Simple Assault based on the failure of the Commonwealth to present any competent evidence that the Defendant committed such an act.
>
> Defense admits they have provided evidence supporting the DUI charge to a prima facie level, but they have failed to do so as to the

---

[188] See *75 Pa.C.S.A. 3801 et seq.*

[189] *18 Pa.C.S. § 2701* "a person is guilty of assault if he: (1) attempts to cause or intentionally, knowingly or recklessly causes bodily injury to another; (2) negligently causes bodily injury to another with a deadly weapon; (3) attempts by physical menace to put another in fear of imminent serious bodily injury; or (4) conceals or attempts to conceal a hypodermic needle on his person and intentionally or knowingly penetrates a law enforcement officer or an officer or an employee of a correctional institution, county jail or prison, detention facility or mental hospital during the course of an arrest or any search of the person."

assault charge. Although the Officer tried to testify about the alleged assault through hearsay, this Court sustained the Defense's objections to that line of testimony. Accordingly they are completely without evidence to sustain their burden of proof on that charge, and I would ask that charge be dismissed."

4.   Attack the charge based on a legal issue.

The Defendant in this case is pulled over by a municipal police officer based on a radio call that was put out by an Officer in a neighbouring municipality. The Officer in the neighbouring municipality allegedly observed a hit and run, but did not follow the suspect. The Officer in question did not observe any suspicious conduct, and no exception to the Jurisdictional requirement (such as hot pursuit) was presented. Defense Counsel should consider attacking the legal authority of the Officer to stop and seize the Defendant.

"Your Honour, the Commonwealth has presented hearsay evidence here tonight that the Defendant may have engaged in illegal conduct in a municipality where the arresting Officer admittedly has no jurisdiction. There has been no testimony or evidence to substantiate these allegations, other than the arresting Officer's testimony about what he heard over the police radio. This was not a report he received from his dispatch headquarters, rather it was a report he heard over the open air without any evidence of reliability or accuracy.

Accordingly when the Officer made the vehicle stop of the Defendant in his municipality he had observed no violation of the motor vehicle law, and was acting without lawful authority as the alleged violation, if it occurred at all, occurred in another jurisdiction. There has been no evidence here tonight to establish hot pursuit or some other exception to the Jurisdictional Act, and accordingly there is no authority for the Officer to have made the arrest.

Defense therefore requests that this Honourable Court dismiss all charges at this time."

Defense Counsel is encouraged to experiment with other possible attacks on the Commonwealth's case during closing.

7

OUTCOME OF THE PRELIMINARY HEARING

§ 7-1   Dismissal

If Defense Counsel is successful in establishing that the Commonwealth has not met its burden of proof to a prima facie level, then the Magisterial District Justice is mandated to dismiss the charges against the Defendant.   This decision is to be publically pronounced at the conclusion of testimony and argument.[190]

The Commonwealth has no right to appeal a determination that *a prima facie* case has not been proven.[191] However, it is permissible for the Commonwealth to refile charges.[192] This is not a double jeopardy issue, as jeopardy does not attach at a Preliminary Hearing.[193] Hopefully, the Commonwealth will be more reasonable in proposing a plea agreement should the decision to refile be made.

There are at least two situations in which the District Attorney may recommend a discharge to the Court, upon the satisfaction of the parties, or a withdrawal of the charges.

§ 7-2   Upon Satisfaction of the Parties

The first situation concerns where the charges are dismissed upon the satisfaction or agreement of all parties.[194] This is provided for only in those cases where the most serious charge is a misdemeanor, and the following conditions are met:

---

[190] *Pennsylvania Rule of Criminal Procedure 543(a)*

[191] *Commonwealth v. Hetherington 460 Pa. 17, 331 A.2d 205 (1975)*

[192] *Rule 544*

[193] *Commonwealth v. Hetherington, 460 Pa. 17, 331 A.2d 205 (1975)* An issuing authority does not attempt to definitely determine the guilt of the accused at a preliminary hearing, thus double jeopardy does not attach where the issuing authority dismisses the charges against the accused. See also *Liciaga v. Court of Common Pleas, 523 Pa. 258, 269 (Pa. 1989)*

[194] *Rule 546*

1. The public interest will not be adversely affected,[195]
2. The affiant or District Attorney consents to the dismissal,[196]
3. The complainant or aggrieved party has been satisfied or made whole,[197] AND
4. There is an agreement as to who shall pay the Court costs.[198]

Such a dismissal is a complete dismissal of all charges, including summary offenses.[199]

This motion is typically made orally at the time of the preliminary hearing, and is sometimes the result of "bad check" cases, small value theft cases, and other misdemeanor offenses, where the complainant is satisfied. A felony may not be withdrawn in such a manner,[200], however, if the felony is withdrawn pursuant to Rule 551 then the remaining misdemeanor or summary charges may be disposed of by such a dismissal. Note that there is no right of a District Justice to modify any of the charges sua sponte.

> "Under the Rules of Criminal Procedure, there is no right in the district justice to change any of the charges. At the preliminary hearing, the district justice's job is merely to determine the existence or non-existence of a prima facie case... The [rules do] not prohibit the district justice from dismissing the case if a

---

[195] *Rule 546(1)*
[196] *Rule 546(2)*
[197] *Rule 546(3)*
[198] *Rule 546(4)*
[199] *Rule 546 Comment*
[200] *Rule 546*

prima facie case is not established; **it simply prohibits *reduction* or *modification* of the original charges.** While one could view a dismissal of the charges as the ultimate reduction, we do not think that the legislature intended such an interpretation[201]." [emphasis added]

So while a District Justice may not reduce or modify the charges against a Defendant, there is no prohibition against a dismissal if a prima facie case is not established. Such a prohibition against reducing or modifying the charges is not violative of separation of powers doctrine[202].

PRACTICE TIP
If a client intends to make the victim whole in a retail theft or bad check case, consider having the victim or victim's counsel sign an affidavit upon acceptance of the funds that no other payment is due. A letter on the victim's counsel's letterhead will also suffice.[203]   DO NOT ask for a letter "withdrawing charges" or agreeing not to "press charges". Such a decision is for the agents of the Commonwealth. The only relevant question is whether all costs have been paid and the victim is made whole.

---

[201] *Commonwealth v. Hernandez 339 Pa.Super. 32, 488 A.2d 293 Pa.Super.,1985.*

[202] *Commonwealth v. Dougherty. 351 Pa. Super. 603, 506 A.2d 936 (1986).*

[203] See *Appendix 17* for a sample affidavit of satisfaction

> Defense Counsel should not fear "admitting guilt" by making such payment. As a remedial action, the act is not normally admissible as evidence at trial. Additionally, if simple mistake is the Client's defense theory (as in the merchandise was thought to have been paid for, or the Defendant did not realize there were insufficient funds in the checking account) then making prompt payment as soon as it is brought to the Defendant's attention may support such a theory.

§ 7-3 Withdrawal

The other method for discharge before the Court is outlined in *Rule 551* and constitutes a withdrawal of the charges. Such a withdrawal must be in writing.[204] The withdrawal may be as to all the charges, or only to some of the charges. Note that unlike *Rule 546,* which provides for dismissal upon the satisfaction of the parties, a withdrawal may be made upon the recommendation of the Attorney for the Commonwealth, and the complainant's satisfaction is not required.

Such withdrawals are sometimes made in cases of questionable merit or where alternative means of satisfaction are available. For example, in cases which are better handled by a civil Protection from Abuse order, or by means of civil suit to recover property to which the ultimate ownership rights are not clear.

---

[204] *Rule 551*

> **PRACTICE TIP**
> How should Defense Counsel proceed with allegations of domestic abuse where both criminal charges and a Protection from Abuse Complaint have been filed? Which hearing should occur first? Is Defense Counsel attached to both matters? Must there be some coordination with other counsel?
> Defense Counsel should be prepared to argue to the Magisterial District Justice and the Commonwealth that the criminal charges should be dismissed if there is a PFA proceeding involving the same parties. This remedy is a better means of resolving the issues, and will not unnecessarily burden the Courts.
> Alternatively, Defense Counsel may wish to ask for a withdrawal based upon an agreement not to contest the PFA action. This entirely depends upon the wishes of the client, and his or her preference for civil or criminal adjudication.

Note that the withdrawal form is required of the commonwealth, not the Defendant.

§ 7-4 Summary Charges joined with other offenses

Normally at a District Court hearing, the Justice may pronounce the guilt or innocence of those charged with summary offenses, and even impose sentence immediately. However, where the right to summary trial intersects with the need for a

Preliminary hearing, there is a conflict.[205] In such cases, where a prima facie case as to any of the misdemeanor, felony or murder charges is sustained, the District Justice is not permitted to adjudicate or dispose of the summary offenses.[206] Rather, the summary offense should be treated as if it is only being considered on a prima facie basis and should be forwarded to the Court of Common Pleas along with the remaining charges.[207]

Should the Commonwealth fail to establish a prima facie case as to all the misdemeanor, felony or murder charges, and the Commonwealth indicates an intention not the refile such charges, the District Justice should determine the Defendant's guilt or innocence as to the summary offenses as if same were presented as part of a summary trial.[208] This is also the case should the more serious charges be withdrawn by the Commonwealth.[209]

Note that it is not entirely clear from these rules whether or not the summary charges must be held for trial regardless of their basis in fact. While guilt beyond a reasonable doubt need not be established to bind the summary charges over for Court, if the Commonwealth is unable to establish prima facie evidence as to the existence of the summary offenses, it is not clear if same may be dismissed or if it should be held for trial regardless. There appears to be inconsistent application of this rule throughout the Commonwealth at this time, as there is no appellate case addressing this issue.

Why would this matter? In certain cases, a Defendant might have more to be concerned about the result of a summary offense than of a misdemeanor offense. For example, a Driving

---

[205] *Rule 543(F)*
[206] *Rule 543(f)(1)*
[207] *Rule 543(f)1*
[208] *Rule 543(f)2, and Rule 454*
[209] *Rule 543(f)(3)*

Under Suspension, DUI related charge[210] is a summary offense that can potentially result in mandatory jail time. Should the client face both the Driving Under Suspension charge, and a minor misdemeanor for which he or she is unlikely to face jail time, it would be more important to the Defendant to dispose of the summary charge than the misdemeanor. If Counsel can establish the fact that a prima facie case as to the summary charge was not established, then it should be argued to the District Justice in the hopes of a dismissal.

§ 7-5 Guilty Pleas

The District Justice is further empowered to accept a plea of guilty to third degree misdemeanors provided that certain conditions are met.[211] Specifically, the misdemeanor must not be a reduced charge,[212] any resultant personal injury or property damage totals less than $500,[213] none of the provisions of the Juvenile act apply,[214] and further provided that the offense does not relate to concealing the death of a child,[215] failure to pay child support,[216] unlawfully listening to the deliberations of a jury,[217] or committing an offense under Title 34 (related to wildlife and game).[218]

---

[210] *75 Pa. C.S.A. § 1543(b)(1)* "...be guilty of a summary offense and shall be sentenced to pay a fine of $ 500 and to undergo imprisonment for a period of **not less than 60 days** nor more than 90 days." [emphasis added]
[211] *42 Pa.C.S.A. 1515(6)(i)*
[212] *42 Pa.C.S.A. 1515(6)(i)(A)*
[213] *42 Pa.C.S.A. 1515(6)(i)(B)*
[214] *42 Pa.C.S.A. 1515(6)(i)(C)*
[215] *42 Pa.C.S.A. 1515(6)(i)(D)*
[216] *42 Pa.C.S.A. 1515(6)(i)(D)*
[217] *42 Pa.C.S.A. 1515(6)(i)(D)*
[218] *42 Pa.C.S.A. 1515(6.1)*

In the case of a first offense DUI,[219] the District Justice may also accept a plea of guilty[220] provided that no personal injury (other than to the Defendant) resulted from the offense,[221] that any property damage (other than to the Defendant's property) was limited to $500 or less,[222] and that the Juvenile act does not apply.[223] For purposes of licensing issues (including possible suspensions) the Magisterial District Justice is further directed to forward the violation to the Clerk of Courts.[224]

Defense Counsel should confer with the District Justice and the Commonwealth regarding the possibility of some kind of Accelerated Rehabilitative Disposition (ARD) or other types of diversionary programs before entering into such a guilty plea. Any potential charges that arise from the same incident and may be filed subsequently should also be considered.[225] This guilty plea may be entered into at any time up to and including the completion of the preliminary hearing.[226]

PRACTICE TIP

Depending on the particulars of Defendant's case, including his criminal history, BAC level, state of license issuance, and desire to remain local for an extended probation term, he or she may be better off pleading guilty to the

---

[219] *75 Pa.C.S.A. 3802*
[220] *42 Pa.C.S.A. 1515(5)*
[221] *42 Pa.C.S.A. 1515(5)(ii)*
[222] *42 Pa.C.S.A. 1515(5)(iv)*
[223] *42 Pa.C.S.A. 1515(5)(v)*
[224] *42 Pa.C.S.A. 1515(5)(vi)*
[225] *Rule 550 Comment* and See *Commonwealth v. Campana, 452 Pa. 233, 304 A.2d 432 (1973), vacated and remanded, 414 U.S. 808 (1973), on remand, 455 Pa. 622, 314 A.2d 854 (1974)*
[226] *Rule 550 Comment*

> DUI at the prelim rather than going through with an ARD program.
>
> Defense Counsel contemplating recommending such an action to his or her client should carefully consider the Defendant's rights, and the effects of the guilty plea. A memo to the client outlining the relative merits of a guilty plea vs. entry into an ARD program will protect Counsel against later recriminations.

In cases where a guilty plea is appropriate, the Magisterial District Justice is required to adhere to the typical requirements of a guilty plea at any level. Specifically, the plea must be in writing,[227] and must be signed by the Defendant with a representation that the plea is entered into knowingly, voluntarily and intelligently.[228] Additionally, the District Justice is directed to perform a full inquiry of the Defendant that the plea is entered into with such considerations.[229] Defense Counsel is strongly advised to ensure his or her client fully understands the ramifications of entering a guilty plea before the District Justice, and should only do so when satisfied that the requirements for a knowing and voluntary plea have been met. For the full protection of the client, and of Defense Counsel, a written guilty plea colloquy should be prepared and tendered at

---

[227] *Rule 550(c)*

[228] *Rule 550(c)(1)*

[229] *Rule 550(b) and (c) 2.* See also *Commonwealth v. Jannetta 413 Pa.Super. 334, 605 A.2d 386 Pa.Super.,1992.* See *Rule 590* and the Comment thereto for further elaboration of the required colloquy. See also *Commonwealth v. Minor, 467 Pa. 230, 356 A.2d 346 (1976), overruled on other grounds in Commonwealth v. Minarik, 493 Pa. 573, 427 A.2d 623, 627 (1981); Commonwealth v. Ingram, 455 Pa. 198, 316 A.2d 77 (1974); Commonwealth v. Martin, 445 Pa. 49, 282 A.2d 241 (1971)*

the time of the plea.[230] If a Court Reporter is present, transcribing the colloquy and plea is also recommended.

There is no requirement that the Defendant be represented by counsel as part of such a plea, however the Defendant should be advised as to his or her right to counsel, and the matter should be treated as a Court case for the procedures regarding appointment of counsel[231]. The Defendant must knowingly and intelligently waive his or her right to counsel.

Of course, Defendants are afforded special protection in such situations, and may, up to 10 days after sentence, change his or her plea to not guilty by notifying the District justice in writing.[232] There is no requirement that the Defendant present good cause for such a change. In such circumstances, the case should proceed to Court as though the charges had been bound over.[233]

§ 7-6   Waiver of Preliminary Hearing

Alternatively, the criminal defendant has the right to waive the preliminary hearing, so long as he or she is represented by counsel.[234] This waiver may be made at the time of the preliminary arraignment or at any subsequent time.[235] If the defendant is not represented by counsel, a waiver may not be made at the time of the preliminary arraignment.[236] A defendant may waive the preliminary hearing, even if he or she is without

---

[230] See Appendix 12 for a sample guilty plea colloquy
[231] *Rule 550 Comment (c)*
[232] *550(d)*
[233] *550(d)*
[234] *Rule 541(a)*
[235] *Id*
[236] *Rule 541(b)*

counsel, at a time subsequent, unless there is a showing of prejudice or manifest injustice.[237]

In those cases where the Defendant waives the preliminary hearing the charges are automatically bound over for court.[238] Such a waiver must be in writing, and should contain certification that the Defendant was apprised of his right to the hearing, but that a knowing and voluntary waiver was made.[239] There is no Commonwealth wide form for the waiver,[240] and each local District Justice's Office should have a form available which will in some manner resemble *Appendix 14,* a sample *Preliminary Hearing Waiver form.*

§ 7-6.1 Why Waive?

Considering the possible benefits which a Defendant may reap, including preservation of issues, testimony, and possible dismissal, under what conditions, if any, should there be a waiver? Counsel should consider the following circumstances, and be prepared to recommend a waiver if it is in the client's best interests.

1. The locality requires waiver to qualify for ARD or some other pre-adjudicative program.

Many local District Attorneys now require Defendants to waive Preliminary Hearings to qualify for ARD. While this practice is offensive to the fair application of the criminal justice system, there is little Defense Counsel can do at this time in opposition. Pennsylvania Courts have consistently held that the

---

[237] *Commonwealth v. Geiger. 455 Pa. 420, 316 A.2d 881 (1974)*
[238] *Rule 541(c)*
[239] *Id*
[240] *Rule 541 Comment*

District Attorney's Office has near unlimited discretion over which Defendants to recommend for ARD or other such programs.[241] To properly prepare for this contingency Counsel should review this option with the client well before the time of the Hearing. Explain that this charge may qualify for ARD, and that if he/she is willing to waive the hearing the District Attorney may agree to recommend him/her for that program.

PRACTICE TIP

Some jurisdictions promise "No deals" if a hearing is held. While this is mostly bluster, there is occasionally some truth to these claims, and it is entirely possible this method of preventing Defendants from exercising their rights to a preliminary hearing may come back into fashion. Familiarity with local procedure or contact with an experienced Public Defender or other local counsel can be invaluable here.

---

2.   The Commonwealth is willing to withdraw or dismiss some of the charges.

Perhaps such a withdrawal would allow the client to apply for the ARD program as above, or it would remove a violent felony, or second offense from the Information.

---

[241] See for example, *Commonwealth v. Sohnleitner, 884 A.2d 307 at 313, Pa.Super.,2005.* "The decision to submit a case for ARD rests in the sound discretion of the district attorney, and absent an abuse of that discretion involving some criteria for admission to ARD 'wholly, patently and without doubt unrelated to the protection of society or the likelihood of a person's success in rehabilitation, such as race, religion or other such obviously prohibited considerations, the attorney for the Commonwealth must be free to submit it for ARD consideration based on his view of what is most beneficial for society and the offender.' *Lutz, supra at 310, 495 A.2d at 935.*"

Whatever the case, there may be such situations in which it would be of tremendous benefit to the client to have some specific charge removed, but this can only be done after careful consultation, and fully informed consent.   Giving up the Preliminary Hearing can be a harsh blow to a criminal defense case, so it should not be given away lightly.

3.   The Commonwealth is willing to agree to a reduced bail in exchange for waiver.

Securing evidence and locking down testimony is an excellent goal, but if the client continues to wallow in the hoosgau pending trial he/she is likely to resent Counsel for it. In these cases, and when it is of significant importance to the client, it may be possible to have the Commonwealth agree to a reduced bail in exchange for the waiver.

4.   The parties have worked out a compromise with which the client is satisfied.

Sometimes the Commonwealth is prepared to enter into a reasonable plea agreement, without further consideration. Of course, the charges need to be waived into Court where the client will eventually plead and the compromise will take effect. In such cases, and where Defense Counsel is confident no further surprises will come about, a waiver may be in the client's best interests. However, be aware of the client's **full criminal background history**[242] so as to prevent additional surprises at

---

[242] Applications for a criminal background history can be obtained through the Pennsylvania State Police by submitting form SP-164 or through the website at: http://www.psp.state.pa.us/psp/cwp/view.asp?A=4&Q=48275. Defense Counsel should take caution to note that this report will only return the client's Pennsylvania Criminal Background. Other jurisdictions are not covered, and may very well turn up during a pre-sentence investigation report. The Defendant should therefore bring every criminal issue to Counsel's attention.

sentencing. Assume that the Pre-Sentencing Reporting process will reveal any defects in the client's past and be prepared for any affect that might have on his or her prior record score.

§ 7-6.2 Procedure for Waiver

Whatever the reason for the waiver, in addition to completing the waiver form required[243] Defense Counsel should consider making a short statement in front of the District Justice to be taken by the Court Reporter. In this statement Counsel should lay out the reasons for the waiver, and explain that the client has been advised as to the consequences of the waiver.

> **PRACTICE TIP**
> "Your Honour, I have reviewed the Affidavit of Probable Cause and the Criminal Complaint with my client and after careful consultation he/she has agreed to waive the charges against him into Court. In exchange for this waiver, the Commonwealth has agreed to withdraw Charges X and Y, or agreed to recommend a reduced bail in the amount of $Z, or agreed to consider the Defendant for application in to the ARD program."

This presents evidence that Counsel has acted in a competent and professional manner should there ever be a question as to what services have been provided for the client.

Also, Counsel should be sure to impress upon the client that the information he provides must be accurate if Counsel is

---

[243] *Rule 541(c)*

to intelligently make a determination as to whether to waive the hearing or not. It does Counsel and the client no good to waive through a DUI charge for ARD if the client conceals from you that he/she has a prior offense in another jurisdiction. Law enforcement and the Commonwealth may not catch it at the time of a Preliminary hearing, especially if it is from another jurisdiction, but it is likely that the ARD department will perform a thorough criminal background check, and it will not slip through the cracks.

§ 7-6.3 Previously Waived by Prior Counsel

Of course, there is also the situation where another attorney has waived the prelim for reasons that are unclear, and new Counsel appears. All is not lost, a Request for Remand as part of the Omnibus Pre-Trial Motions can be filed which asks the Court to either hear the issue on prima facie evidence directly, or send the case back to the District Court for a new hearing.[244]

PRACTICE TIP

Defense Counsel should ensure there wasn't a negotiated agreement in place that would be invalidated by such a motion. Defense Counsel should contact prior counsel or the District Attorney's Office directly for additional details.[245]

---

[244] See *Appendix 19* for a sample Motion asking the Court to return the case to the Magisterial District Justice

[245] See *Appendix 7* for a letter entering appearance previously represented by another attorney.

§ 7-7   Held for Court

In those cases where the charges are held for Court following the Preliminary Hearing, the Magisterial District Justice is directed to file the appropriate paperwork with the Clerk of Courts for further hearing, trial, or other disposition.[246] If the Defendant was not previously fingerprinted and processed the Magisterial District Justice should set such an order at this time.

In those cases where the Magisterial District Justice forwards an incorrect record of the proceedings of the preliminary hearing,[247] there is a procedure to provide for the correction of these records.[248] In such cases, the concerned party should file an application with the Court of Common Pleas[249] to perfect the record to conform to the facts of the case.[250] The party claiming to be aggrieved by the defect has burden of correcting it.[251] In such cases, the Stenographer's Transcript is invaluable.

§ 7-8   Bail

In those circumstances where the charges against the Defendant are held for Court the District Justice is directed to set bail if it has not already been set at a preliminary arraignment.[252] If bail has already been set then the District Justice may continue

---

[246] *Rule 547*

[247] For example, if the paperwork indicates the wrong charges have been bound for Court, or an incorrect bail amount has been recorded.

[248] *Rule 548*

[249] See *Appendix 20*, Motion to Correct Transcript

[250] *Id*

[251] *Commonwealth v. Trivelli, 384 A.2d 962, 253 Pa.Super. 34, Super.1978.*

[252] *Rule 543(c)(1)*

the existing order, or upon good cause shown may modify the bail.[253]

The District Justice may modify the bail at any time up to and including the conclusion of the Preliminary Hearing.[254] Additionally, it may be modified at any time by a judge of the court of common pleas.[255] Once the Court of Common Pleas has set bail, it may not be further modified by the District Justice.[256] If counsel is unsatisfied with the bail as set by the District Justice, an expedited motion to the court of common pleas should be his or her next step.[257]

There are several types of bail available to the criminal defendant.[258] This includes:

1.   Release on Recognizance (ROR). This type of bail provides that the Defendant may be released conditioned only upon the defendant's written agreement to appear when required and to comply with the rules of the bail bond such as refraining from further criminal conduct.

2.   Release on Nonmonetary Conditions. Additional nonmonetary conditions can be set, such as a prohibition on Defendant leaving the jurisdiction, an order to refrain from having contact with the victim, or an agreement to vacate premises (in cases of domestic abuse).

---

[253] *Rule 543(c)2 and 529*
[254] *Rule 529(a) and (b)*
[255] *Rule 529(c)*
[256] *Rule 529(d)*
[257] See *Appendix 21*, Modification of Bail Request
[258] *234 PA Code 524*

3.   Release on Unsecured Bail Bond. The Defendant pledges to be responsible for a set figure if he or she fails to appear as required. No money is deposited, and as long as the Defendant appears at all future Court appearances this will have no effect on his or her finances.

4.   Release on Nominal Bail. The Court may require a minimal deposit, and accept the agreement of a third person, organization or bail agency to act as surety for the defendant. This needs to be coordinated with the bail agency and often requires the posting of a person's real property interest.

5.   Release on a Monetary Condition. The Defendant's release requires the posting of a financial deposit to ensure later appearance. This also may need to be coordinated with a bail agency and may require the Defendant to post a significant sum or title to property.

PRACTICE TIP

Defense Counsel should have the contact information for a reliable local bail agency on file to provide to criminal defendants. Counsel should also inquire about the agency's posting requirements, and know ahead of time what costs are involved for defendants.

At the conclusion of the Preliminary Hearing, if the client was previously unable to make bail, now is the time to argue for a bail reduction. While this is obviously easier if the Commonwealth consents to same, it is by no means impossible even in the face of opposition. Many District Justices respect that retaining an attorney indicates a Defendant's increased likelihood to remain in the jurisdiction for future proceedings, and may modify bail on that basis alone. Of course, the normal bail arguments including ties to the community, length of residency, employment, familial obligations, and other issues are relevant at this time[259].

---

[259] See *Rule 523(a)*, which reviews the relevant release criteria and includes "all available information as that information is relevant to the defendant's appearance or nonappearance at subsequent proceedings, or compliance or noncompliance with the conditions of the bail bond". It further specifies several pertinent factors. Note that the decision of the Defendant note to deny guilt is NOT a factor to be held against him or her in considering the application of bail. *523(b)*.

8

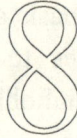

POST-PRELIMINARY HEARING
AND CONCLUSION

122

§ 8-1   Decision of District Justice

The Decision of a District Justice to bind the charges over for Court is not directly appealable.

> "There is, however, no legal procedure, such as certiorari, for supervision of the correctness of the proceedings before the justice of the peace. There is the writ of habeas corpus for illegal confinement [citations omitted]. There are few means of direct attack upon defective proceedings before the justice of the peace [citations omitted]. His is not a court of record, and the transcript furnishes no record adequate for detailed review [citations omitted]. For precise recognition and implementation of rights, the accused must look to the de novo proceedings in the Common Pleas Court. He is thus assured of nonconviction unless and until all essential proofs are made and essential procedures are followed. The limited function of the preliminary hearing, and its imperfections, must be recognized."[260]

Defense counsel thus aggrieved with an erroneous decision by a District Justice should then look to the Court of Common Pleas and file a petition for writ of habeas corpus[261]. The writ of habeas corpus is the proper means for testing a pre-

---

[260] *Commonwealth v. Mitchell, 1975 Pa. Dist. & Cnty. Dec. LEXIS 293 (Pa. C.P. 1975) citing Commonwealth v. Gipson, 28 Somerset 192 (1972); Colten v. Kentucky, 407 U.S. 104, 92 S. Ct. 1953, 32 L. Ed. 2d 584, 593 (1972).*
[261] See *Appendix 23* for a sample OPTM asserting Habeas Corpus relief.

trial finding that the Commonwealth has sufficient evidence to establish a prima facie case.[262] At such a habeas hearing, the underlying issue is limited to determining if the Commonwealth has presented sufficient evidence to establish a prima facie case.[263] The trial court cannot make credibility and weight determinations.[264]

In those cases where testimony was taken at the preliminary hearing, Defense Counsel should still consider filing such a motion, as it will provide a second opportunity to examine witnesses. In such cases Counsel will have a better expectation of testimony and a better understanding of the legal issues at play. Alternatively, to save time and expense, the transcript taken at the time of the Preliminary Hearing may be introduced as an exhibit to the Court, with heavy citations thereto in Counsel's brief, of course.

§ 8-2 Filing of Information

If some or all of the charges against the Defendant are bound over for Court then the District Attorney is required to prepare an information and file it with the Court of Common Pleas.[265] The contents of the information are regulated by the Rules of Criminal Procedure, and provide some details as to the specifics of the offenses and how they relate to the criminal charges.[266]

The Defendant is entitled to a copy of the Information after filing.[267] The general rule in Pennsylvania is that the

---

[262] *Commonwealth v. Hendricks, 927 A.2d 289 Pa.Super.,2007*
[263] *Commonwealth v. Williams, 911 A.2d 548 Pa.Super.,2006*
[264] *Id*
[265] *Rule 560*
[266] *Rule 560, A-D*
[267] *Rule 562*

accused must be held to the next term of court following the Preliminary Hearing.[268]

PRACTICE TIP

Although local practice in most jurisdictions is to forward a copy of the Information to Defense Counsel as soon as it is filed, some may wait until the Arraignment, or until discovery begins. In such cases, if Defense Counsel is concerned about the accuracy of the official transcript he or she should contact the Clerk of Courts for a certified copy of the transcript as soon as it has been filed.

The only certain resource for Counsel to examine the official transcript is by personally visiting the local Clerk of Courts' Office and physically inspecting the file. However, there are also several alternatives available when such a visit is not practical. Many local Court systems are now putting complete criminal dockets online, and a summarized version of the information can be obtained through the UJS service.[269]

---

§ 8-3   Reinstituting Charges

Even when Counsel is fortunate enough to obtain a dismissal or convince the Commonwealth to withdraw the charges, the case is not necessarily completed. The

---

[268] *P.L.E. Criminal Law Sec 181,* citing *Commonwealth v. Nelson, 34 Erie 235, (1951).*

[269] http://ujsportal.pacourts.us/

Commonwealth is permitted in such cases to refile the charges with the same Magisterial District Justice.[270] As an Magisterial District Justice's decision to dismiss criminal charges is an unappealable decision, the only means available to the Commonwealth is to seek such a refiling.[271] Such a refiling may be opposed by the Defendant[272] only in those circumstances where there is evidence of a pattern of prosecutorial harassment[273], or the applicable statute of limitations[274] has expired. [275]

Additionally, the Commonwealth may choose to refile the charges before a different Magisterial District Justice.[276]

§ 8-4   Conclusion

The Preliminary Hearing is an important check on the criminal justice system for Defendants, and a valuable tool in attacking the Commonwealth's case for Defense Counsel. A keen understanding of the relevant rules will ensure that Counsel is in a position to take full advantage of the protections offered by the Preliminary Hearing.

Also it is worth noting that the Preliminary Hearing can contribute to the relationship between the client and the attorney. Seeing someone fight for his or her rights can have a profound

---

[270] *Rule 544(A)*, also *Comment*. As to the Authority of the Commonwealth to reinstutute the charges see *McNair's Petition, 187 A. 498 (Pa. 1936); Commonwealth v. Thorpe, 701 A.2d 488 (Pa. 1997)*.

[271] *Commonwealth v. Carbo, 822 A.2d 60, Super.2003.*

[272] See *Appendix 22* for a sample Motion to Quash Refiling of charges.

[273] *Stewart v. Abraham, C.A.3 (Pa.)2001, 275 F.3d 220, certiorari denied 122 S.Ct. 2661, 536 U.S. 958, 153 L.Ed.2d 836.*

[274] See *42 Pa.C.S. § 5551-5554* for more information on the applicable statute of limitations.

[275] *Rule 544 Comment* and *Commonwealth v. Thorpe, 701 A.2d 488 (Pa. 1997)*

[276] *Rule 544(b) and Rule 132.*

effect on the client's attitude. Even if unsuccessful in having the charges dismissed, Defense Counsel may find that a client can be satisfied that a zealous defense was offered. Conversely, if Defense Counsel does not satisfy the client's desire for what he or she perceives as justice, even if the result is successful, the client may be dissatisfied. Perhaps going so far as to contest the payment of legal fees, or attacking the attorney's reputation in the community.

The best method to prevent such negative results is to adequately prepare for the preliminary hearing. As this guide has demonstrated that means more than just studying up on the statutes of the crimes charged. It means knowing the procedural rules in place, both Commonwealth wide and locality specific. It means being familiar with the likely issues which will arise, both legal and practical. And it means preparing the client with realistic expectations for the hearing.

APPENDICES

The following forms, samples, and suggested documents contain the bare minimum information required for most jurisdictions in the Commonwealth, but are not tailored to any particular set of local rules. Competent representation of a client requires that Counsel check the local rules for additional filing instructions.

The proposed orders attached to these documents may also have to be modified depending on local procedure. Many jurisdictions require specific motions to be presented at specific locations (for example, presenting Bail Modification Requests to the Court Administrator's Office rather than the Clerk of Courts). These local procedural requirements may not be set forth in the written local rules, and so Counsel is urged to contact the relevant offices involved to determine how best to proceed.

When contacting these offices, it is always best to receive a copy of the local procedures in writing. Some offices will be kind enough to fax or mail a copy of these rules to Defense Counsel. However, on other occasions only an oral representation as to the local procedure can be made. In such circumstances, cautious Counsel will note the contact name and information of the person or office involved in the client's file. Note that ignorance of local procedure is rarely a successful defense to a Post-Conviction Relief Act claim. If Counsel is not able to adequately prepare him or herself for action in an unknown jurisdiction then the best policy is to refer the case to someone who can.

APPENDICES TABLE OF CONTENTS

Appendix 1
Affidavit of Probable Cause and Police Criminal Complaint

Defendants Name: Jane Doe

Docket Number:

POLICE

CRIMINAL COMPLAINT

AFFIDAVIT Of PROBABLE CAUSE

On May 10th, 2007 at approximately 1814 hours, I, Officer Jaime Suarez was dispatched by home County Control Center to the S-Mart in town for a retail theft. Control center further advised that S-Mart Asset Protection Officers were in foot pursuit of the suspects. Several minutes later, Control center advised that the suspects struck another vehicle and fled in a gold GMC SUV, bearing PA registration WNP 0999. A check of the registration showed the vehicle was a 2003 GMC registered to Jane Doe.

At approximately 1825 hours, Officer William Fehringer observed the vehicle and conducted a traffic stop on Forks Street, in Hometown. The Operator was identified as Jane Doe and the front seat passenger was identified as Elizabeth Doe. Officer Fehringer asked Doe what happened at S-Mart. Doe stated that her daughter was trying to take clothes out of the store.

At approximately 1827 hours, I arrived at S-Mart. Upon arrival I spoke with Asset protection Officer Sloane Treat. Treat advised that he observed two females shoplifting items from different sections of the store. Treat advised that both were black females and appeared to be mother and daughter. Treat stated that he observed both suspects place merchandise inside empty S-Mart bags. Treat stated that the two suspects then placed the bags in a shopping cart and attempted to exit the front doors without paying. Treat stated that he stopped the two suspects after they passed the cash registers and identified himself as S-Mart Asset Protection. Treat stated that the two females left the merchandise and the shopping cart and fled out of the store on foot. Treat stated that he chased the two suspects and observed them get into a gold GMC SUV, which was parked on the south side of the building. Treat stated that the GMC backed out of a parking spot and then drove forward, striking him in the leg and a parked vehicle. Treat stated that the vehicle did not stop and left the parking lot.

I then spoke with Marc Kurtz. Kurtz advised that he was the owner of the vehicle that was struck. I then observed a white Mercury Mountaineer bearing PA registration FHY-9886 with damage to the passenger side rear bumper. I then asked Kurtz if he was in the vehicle when it was struck. Kurtz stated that he was not. Kurtz stated that he parked his vehicle and was walking toward the store when he observed a man chasing two females. Kurtz stated that he observed a black female get into a gold SUV and back up. Kurtz stated that the female then drove forward and struck his vehicle. Kurtz stated that the SUV did not stop and continued driving out of the parking lot.

I, _____Officer Jaime Suarez_____ BEING DULY SWORN ACCORDING TO LAW, DEPOSE AND SAY THAT THE FACTS SET FORTH IN THE FOREGOING AFFIDAVIT ARE TRUE AND CORRECT TO THE BEST OF MY KNOWLEDGE, INFORMATION AND BELIEF.

_____
(Signature of Affiant)

Sworn to me and subscribed before me this __11th__ day of __May__, 20 07.

__May, 11th, 2007__ Date   __Wesley Torres__, District Justice

My commission expires first Monday of January, __2012__   SEAL

AOPC (2-82-5)   36

Appendix 1
Affidavit of Probable Cause and Police Criminal Complaint

COMMONWEALTH OF PENNSYLVANIA
COUNTY OF: _Home_

POLICE
CRIMINAL COMPLAINT

COMMONWEALTH OF PENNSYLVANIA
VS.

Magisterial District Number:

District Justice Name: Honorable
Wesley Torres
Address: 124 Poe Street
Hometown, PA 19292

Telephone 717-555-1212

DEFENDANT:
NAME and ADDRESS
Jane Doe
1313 Shiny Mountain Road
Hometown, PA 19292

Docket No: CR -07
Date Filed: 6|20|07
OTN:

District Attorney's Office ☐ Approved ☐ Disapproved because: _____
(The district attorney may require that the complaint, arrest warrant affidavit, or both be approved by the attorney for the Commonwealth prior to filing. PA.R.Cr.P. 107.)

I, _Jaime Suarez_

of, _Hometown Municipal Police Department_

do hereby state: (check the appropriate box)
1. ☒ I accuse the above named defendant who lives at the address set forth above
   ☐ accuse the defendant whose name is unknown to me but who is described as

☐ . accuse the defendant whose name and popular designation or nickname is unknown to me and whom I have therefore designated as John Doe,
with violating the penal laws of the Commonwealth of Pennsylvania at _S-Mart in Hometown_

in _Home_ County on or about: _5-10-07_ at _1814_ hour(s).
Participants were: (if there were participants place their names here repeating the name of above defendant)

2. The acts committed by the accused were:
(Set forth a summary of the facts sufficient to advise the defendant of the nature of the offense charged. A citation to the statute allegedly violated without more, is not sufficient. In a summary case you must cite the specific section and subsection of the statute or ordinance allegedly violated.)

AOPC 412-(596)   1-3

Appendix 1
Affidavit of Probable Cause and Police Criminal Complaint

(continuation of No. 2)

POLICE
CRIMINAL COMPLAINT

Defendant's Name:

Docket Number:

Court# 1- 18 Pa C.S.A. &3929&8:a)(1) Retail Theft (M-1)
(1) A person is guilty of a retail theft if he: takes possession of, carries away, transfers or causes to be carried away or
transferred, any merchandise displayed, held, stored or offered for sale by any store or other retail mercantile
establishment with the intention of depriving the merchant of the possession, use or benefit of such merchandise without
paying the full retail value thereof.

Court # 2 - 18 Pa C.S.A.§630'88(a) Corruption of Minors (M-1)
(1) Whoever, being of the age of 18 years and upwards, by any act corrupts or tends to corrupt the morals of any minor
less than 18 years of age, or who aids, abets, entices or encourages any such minor in the commission of any crime, or
who knowingly assists or encourages such minor in violating his or her parole or any order of the court, commits a
misdemeanor of the first degree.

all of which were against the peace and dignity of the Commonwealth of Pennsylvania and contrary to the Act
of Assembly, or in violation of

1.	3929	a	1	of the	18
	(Section)	(Subsection)			(Pa Statue)	(counts)
2.	5301	a 1	of the	18	1
	(Section)	(Subsection)		(Pa Statue)	(counts)
3.	2705		of the	18	1
	(Section)	(Subsection)		(Pa Statue)	(counts)
4.	3745	a	of the	75	1
	(Section)	(Subsection)		(Pa Statue)	(counts)
5.			of the		
	(Section)	(Subsection)		(Pa Statue)	(counts)

3. I ask that a warrant of arrest or a summons be issued and that the accused be required to answer the charges I have
made. (In order for a warrant of arrest to issue, the attached affidavit of probable cause must be completed
and sworn to before the issuing authority.)

4. I verify that the facts set forth in this complaint are true and correct to the best of my knowledge or information and
belief. This verification is made subject to the penalties of Section 4904 of the Crimes Code (18 PA. C.S. § 4904) relating
to unsworn falsification to authorities.

19 June , 20 07 _____
(Signature of Affiant)

AND NOW, on this date 19 June , 2007 I certify that the complaint has been properly
completed and verified. An affidavit of probable cause must be completed in order for a warrant to issue.

_____   _____ SEAL
(Magisterial District)   (Issuing Authority)

AOPC 412/6/98   2-1

132

APPENDICES

Appendix 1
Affidavit of Probable Cause and Police Criminal Complaint

(continuation of No. 2)

POLICE
CRIMINAL COMPLAINT

Defendant's Name:

Docket Number:

Count # 3   18 Pa §2705 Recklessly Endangering Another Person (Misdemeanor 2)
In that the defendant did knowingly and recklessly engage in conduct which placed or may have placed another person, in danger of death or serious bodily injury.

Count # 4   75 Pa §3745 (a) Accidents Involving Damage to Unattended Vehicle or Property (Summary)
In that the actor did drive and/or operate a motor vehicle upon a highway or trafficway within this Commonwealth, which was involved in an accident with any vehicle or other property which was unattended, resulting in damage to the vehicle or property.

all of which was against the peace and dignity of the Commonwealth of Pennsylvania and contrary to the Act of Assembly, or in violation of

1.			of the		
(Section)	(Subsection)			(Pa Statue)	(counts)
2.			of the		
(Section)	(Subsection)			(Pa Statue)	(counts)
3.			of the		
(Section)	(Subsection)			(Pa Statue)	(counts)
4.			of the		
(Section)	(Subsection)			(Pa Statue)	(counts)
5.			of the		
(Section)	(Subsection)			(Pa Statue)	(counts)

3.   I ask that a warrant of arrest or a summons be issued and that the accused be required to answer the charges I have made. (In order for a warrant of arrest to issue, the attached affidavit of probable cause must be completed and sworn to before the issuing authority.)

4.   I verify that the facts set forth in this complaint are true and correct to the best of my knowledge or information and belief. This verification is made subject to the penalties of Section 4904 of the Crimes Code (18 PA. C.S. § 4904) relating to unsworn falsification to authorities.

_____ _B. June_____ , 20 _07_   _____
                                                              (Signature of Affiant)

AND NOW, on this date _____ _19 June_____ , 20 _07_, I certify that the complaint has been properly completed and verified. An affidavit of probable cause must be completed in order for a warrant to issue.

                                                                            ... SEAL

_____   _____
(Magisterial District)   (Issuing Authority)

AOPC 412 (6/98)   2-3

133

Appendix 2
Preliminary Hearing Checklist

___Review Affidavit of Probable Cause
Possible Pre-Trial or Suppression Issues:

_____

_____

_____

___Contact the District Justice's Office
___Entry of Appearance filed
___Continuance requested (if necessary)
___Contact Police Officer
Possible Collateral consequences (license suspension, probation violation, etc.):

_____

_____

_____

___Contact District Attorney
___Appearance letter
ADA Assigned to Case (if known):

_____

___Contact Public Defender's Office (or prior counsel)
Any documents or items required:

_____

_____

_____

___Secure services of Court Reporter
Service and contact information:

_____

_____

_____

Appendix 2
Preliminary Hearing Checklist

___Prepare relevant questions

_____

_____

_____

_____

_____

_____

___Protential legal issues

_____

_____

_____

_____

___Prepare Client
    ___Letter to client with date of hearing
    ___Letter indicating rescheduled date (if continued)
___Subpoena witnesses or documents
    Witness #1 Name and Contact information

_____

_____

    ___Subpoena issued on [Date]
    ___Documents requested (if so, specify same)

_____

_____

    Witness #2 Name and Contact information

_____

_____

_____

Appendix 2
Preliminary Hearing Checklist

___Subpoena issued on [Date]
___Documents requested (if so, specify same)

_____

_____

_____

Additional Notes

_____

_____

_____

_____

_____

_____

_____

_____

_____

_____

_____

_____

APPENDICES

Appendix 3
Entry of Appearance

[Date]

[District Justice]

Re: *Commonwealth of Pennsylvania vs.*
[Defendant]
Docket No.

Dear [District Justice]:

Please be advised this office has been retained to represent [Defendant] in the above captioned matter. It is my understanding that he/she is currently scheduled for a Preliminary Hearing on the [Date]. [Defendant] intends to appear at that time and enter a defense to the charges against him/her.

Thank you.

Sincerely,

[Defense Counsel]

cc: Client
District Attorney

Appendix 4
Pre-Hearing Letter to Police Officer

[Date]

[Officer, Detective, Trooper, etc.]

Re: *Commonwealth of Pennsylvania vs.*
Defendant
Docket No.

Dear [Officer]:

Please be advised that this office has been retained to represent [Defendant] in the above captioned matter currently scheduled for a Preliminary Hearing before [Magisterial District Justice] on or about the [Date of hearing].

[Option 1] It is my understanding that [Defendant] is being charged with a violation of the vehicle code concerning driving under the Influence while incapable of safely driving, and that he is further being charged with refusing the BAC test which you requested of him. This would normally require you to forward the refusal paperwork to PennDot for processing.

[Option 2] It is my understanding that your investigation is ongoing and that [Defendant] may face additional charges arising from the incident in question.

Appendix 4
Pre-Hearing Letter to Police Officer

While I understand there are certain procedures you must follow in these types of cases, I would appreciate it if you would withhold [submitting the refusal paperwork to PennDot] [filing additional charges] until after we have had an opportunity to speak with each other concerning the issues in this case. It is my hope that a resolution can be reached after our discussion.

Sincerely,

[Defense Counsel]

Appendix 5
Pre-hearing letter to Public Defender's Office

[Date]

[Public Defender or Prior Counsel]

Re: *Commonwealth of Pennsylvania vs.*
        [Defendant]
        Docket No.

Dear [Public Defender or Prior Counsel]:

Please be advised that this office has been retained by [Defendant] with regard to the above captioned matter. It is our intention to appear on his behalf at the Preliminary Hearing currently scheduled for [Date] before [Magisterial District Justice], and accordingly your appearance will not be required at that time. If your office is in possession of any evidence or items that would be of assistance to [Defendant] at the time of the Preliminary Hearing, please forward them to my attention as soon as possible.

[If there are specific documents which are known to be in possession of Public Defender's Office then itemize such requests here].

Thank you for your time and attention in this matter.

Sincerely,

[Defense Counsel]

Appendix 6
Pre-hearing letter to District Attorney's Office

[Date]

[District Attorney]

Re: *Commonwealth of Pennsylvania vs.*
      [Defendant]
      Docket No.

Dear [District Attorney]:

Please be advised that this office has been retained by [Defendant] with regard to the above captioned matter. It is my intention to appear on his behalf at the Preliminary Hearing currently scheduled for [Date] before [MDJ] and enter a defense to the charges.

[If ARD eligible: It is my understanding that [Defendant] may be eligible for the ARD program through your office. If this is the case, [Defendant] would consider waiving the charges through to Court upon your office's agreement to recommend him for this program. I would ask that you verify his eligibility through your office in time for the hearing.]

[If specific documentary evidence is required: It is my understanding that your office has in its possession potentially exculpatory evidence in the form of [a statement, a video recording, a chemical test analysis, etc.]. Consider this a request to produce such evidence at the time of the hearing. If you will be unable to produce same at that time, please contact me at this office to arrange a time when I can personally view these items prior to the hearing.]

Appendix 6
Pre-hearing letter to District Attorney's Office

[If a continuance, pre-hearing motion, or other issues are likely to arise, set out specifically what is being requested and whether the concurrence of the District Attorney's Office is necessary.]

Thank you for your time and attention in this matter.

Sincerely,

[Defense Counsel]

Appendix 7
Letter to District Attorney upon Assumption of Representation

[Date]

[Defendant]

Re: *Commonwealth of Pennsylvania vs.*
     Defendant
     Docket No.

Dear [District Attorney]:

Please be advised this Office has been retained to represent [Defendant] with regard to the above captioned criminal charges. It is my understanding that at the time of the Preliminary Hearing this matter was waived into Court by prior counsel. I have received no indications that this waiver was part of a negotiated plea agreement, or that any consideration was made for Defendant for this waiver.

After consultation with my client, and an examination of the relevant evidence in my possession I belive that this waiver was not made in his best interests, or with his full knowledge and consent. Accordingly, I will be filing a Motion with the Court to remand this matter to [MDJ] to determine if prima facie evidence exists to continue this matter.

If you wish to discuss this matter, including potentially negotiating an agreement, feel free to contact me at this office.

Sincerely,

[Defense Counsel]

Appendix 8
Objection to Venue

[CAPTION]
<u>ORDER OF COURT</u>
AND NOW, this _____ day of _____ _____,
upon consideration of Defendant's Motion to Dismiss and
Objection to Venue, it is hereby ORDERED,

1. That the charges against the Defendant are hereby
   dismissed.
2. That venue is properly held before [Magisterial
   District Justice 2]. A Preliminary Hearing shall be
   scheduled as soon as practicable before said
   Magisterial District Judge.

BY THE COURT,

_____

CC: Defense Counsel
     District Attorney
     Magisterial District Justice
     Magisterial District Justice 2

Appendix 8
Objection to Venue

[CAPTION]
MOTION TO DISMISS AND OBJECTION TO VENUE

AND NOW, comes the Defendant, and submits this Motion to Dismiss and Objection to Venue, upon the following:

1.   That on or about [Date], your Petitioner was charged with the commission of the following crimes:

[Specify Charges]

2.   That original charges were filed and issued by the [Magisterial District Justice], who recused herself because of a conflict of interest.

3.   That based upon the recusal of [Magisterial District Justice], the case was reassigned by this Honourable Court to [Magisterial District Justice 2].

4.   That based upon the docket entries entered in the original proceeding, [Magisterial District Justice 2] was the final issuing authority.

5.   That the full Preliminary Hearing, during which twenty one (21) witnesses were called and forty five (45) Exhibits introduced, [Magisterial District Justice 2] dismissed all the charges against your Movant, with the exception of the following, which were bound to over for Court:

[Specify charges]

6.   That the refiling of the criminal charges against your Movant was accomplished through [Magisterial District Justice], who was the issuing authority, notwithstanding the fact that she had previously recused herself.

7.   That pursuant to *Rule 544* of the Pennsylvania Rules of Criminal Procedure, the Commonwealth had the obligation of filing the new charges to the issuing authority who

Appendix 8
Objection to Venue

dismissed the charges, which in this instance meant with [Magisterial District Justice 2].

       8.   That by reason of the aforementioned, the charges were improperly filed and issued by [Magisterial District Justice].

       9.   That the proper procedure to have followed, based upon the Pennsylvania Rules of Criminal Procedure, was for the Commonwealth to refile the charges with [Magisterial District Justice 2] and, if dissatisfied for some reason with [Magisterial District Justice 2], file a Petition with this Honourable Court to have the cases assigned to another Magisterial District Judge.

      18.   That the proper procedure was not followed in this case, which arises to a due process violation, pursuant to Rule 132 of the Pennsylvania Rules of Criminal Procedure.

      19.   That a Preliminary Arraignment was scheduled before [Magisterial District Justice] for [Date] at which time your Movant, as well as her Co-Defendants, did raise the issues set forth herein before [Magisterial District Justice], who declined to dismiss the charges and/or transfer the charges to [Magisterial District Justice 2].

      20.   That Rule 134 of the Pennsylvania Rules of Criminal Procedure permits the filing of Objections to Venue between Magisterial Districts.

      21.   That your Movant has been prejudiced by reason of the fact that her constitutional right to due process has been denied her by virtue of the procedure used, assigning the refiled charges to [Magisterial District Justice].

Appendix 8
Objection to Venue

23.   That in the alternative to the relief requested in Section I of this Motion, venue of the refiled charges should be transferred to [Magisterial District Justice 2].

WHEREFORE, your Movant, pursuant to *Rule 134* of the Pennsylvania Rules of Criminal Procedure, objects to the venue before [Magisterial District Justice] and respectfully requests this Honourable Court to transfer the refiled charges to [Magisterial District Justice 2].

RESPECTFULLY SUBMITTED,

[Defense Counsel]

Appendix 9
Written Agreement to transfer (555(b)1

[CAPTION]
STIPULATION

And now, this [Date], by this written agreement of the parties or their representative, it is stipulated that the above captioned proceedings should be transferred to [Magisterial District Justice] in order to best secure the fair and impartial application of justice.

_____

District Attorney

_____

Defense Counsel

CC: Magisterial District Justice
       Clerk of Courts

APPENDICES

Appendix 10
Objection to Transfer

[CAPTION]
ORDER OF COURT

AND NOW, this _____ day of _____ _____,
upon consideration of Defendant's Objection to Transfer, the
District Attorney's Motion to Transfer is hereby DENIED, and a
preliminary hearing in the above captioned matter shall be held
on the _____ day of _____, _____, at
_____ o'clock ____.m. in District Court No. _____, before the
Honourable [Magisterial District Justice].

BY THE COURT,

_____

cc: Defense Counsel
      District Attorney
      Court Administrator
      Magisterial District Justice

Appendix 10
Objection to Transfer

[CAPTION]
OBJECTION TO COMMONWEALTH'S
PETITION TO TRANSFER

AND NOW, comes the defendant, by his attorneys, and respectfully avers the following:

1. Criminal charges have been filed against [Defendant] in front of [specify Magisterial District Justice].
2. These criminal charges include [specify charges].
3. A Preliminary Hearing is currently scheduled for [date].
4. The Commonwealth has petitioned for a temporary assignment to another Magisterial District Justice. See Exhibit A [attach petition].
5. The Commonwealth has not established that the temporary reassignment is necessary to ensure impartial proceedings pursuant to *PA.R.Crim.P. 132(A)(2)*
6. *Commonwealth v. Kline, 555 A.2d 892, 894 (Pa., 1989)* held that impartial behavior on the part of the issuing authority must be shown in order to grant a motion for temporary assignment of the issuing authority.
7. Under *Commonwealth v. Kline, 555 A.2d 892, 894 (Pa., 1989)* if no impartial behavior is shown, the grant of temporary assignment is an abuse of discretion and grounds for reversal of the grant.

APPENDICES

Appendix 10
Objection to Transfer

WHEREFORE, the defendant respectfully requests this Honourable Court to dismiss the Commonwealth's Motion to assign to another Magisterial District Justice the above named charges.

Respectfully submitted,

[Defense Counsel]

Appendix 11
Motion to Reassign Preliminary Hearing

[CAPTION]

<u>O R D E R</u>

AND   NOW,   this   _____   day   of
_____, _____, upon consideration of
the attached Petition, it is hereby ORDERED that the
Preliminary Hearing previously scheduled in this matter is
reassigned to [Magisterial District Justice] of District Court No.
_____. A Preliminary Hearing to be scheduled by [Magisterial
District Justice] within 10 days hereof.

BY THE COURT:

_____

cc: Defense Counsel
        District Attorney
        Magisterial District Justice
        Court Administrator

APPENDICES

Appendix 11
Motion to Reassign Preliminary Hearing

[CAPTION]
MOTION TO REASSIGN PRELIMINARY HEARING

AND NOW, comes [Defendant] by his attorneys, and respectfully avers the following:

1. [Defendant] is currently charged with [specify charges]
2. [Defendant] is scheduled for a Preliminary Hearing before [Magisterial District Justice] on [specify date]
3. Pa.R.Crim.P.132(a)(2) provides that temporary assignment can be granted to another Magisterial District Justice on the grounds that the assignment is to ensure impartial proceedings.
4. [Defendant] avers that [Magisterial District Justice] will be unable to impartially and fairly administer the proceedings as [specify issue – for example "the Magisterial District Justice is currently involved in a business transaction with Defendant", or "the Magisterial District Justice is closely related to the alleged victim in this matter" or some other legally cognizable conflict of interest"]
5. [Defendant] avers that his rights will be prejudiced if his Preliminary hearing is not administered in a fair and impartial manner.

Appendix 11
Motion to Reassign Preliminary Hearing

WHEREFORE, the defendant respectfully requests this Honourable Court to assign the above captioned case to another Magisterial District Justice within this Court's authority.

Respectfully submitted,

[Defense Counsel]

APPENDICES

Appendix 12
Notice of Preliminary Hearing

COMMONWEALTH OF PENNSYLVANIA
COUNTY OF:

Mag. Dist. No.:

MDJ Name/ Bar.
Erik Peterson

Address: 154 Tintle Ave
Hometown, PA 19292

Telephone:

OFFICER : Trooper Brian Hugenbruch
PSP Brown Ridge
1600 Bellemonte Ave
Hometown, PA 19292

NOTICE OF
PRELIMINARY HEARING

COMMONWEALTH OF

PENNSYLVANIA

VS.
DEFENDANT: NAME and ADDRESS

Jane Doe
1313 Mockingbird Lane
Hometown, PA 19292

Docket No.:
Date Filed:

Charge(s):

S 18 §3929 §§A1 RETAIL THEFT
S 18 §6301 §§A1 CORRUPTION OF MINORS
S 18 §2705 RECKLESSLY ENDANGERING ANOTHER PERSON

NOTICE TO DEFENDANT

A complaint has been filed charging you with the offense(s) set forth above and on the attached copy of the complaint. A preliminary hearing on these charges has been scheduled for:

Date:	Place:
	[District Justice's Address, or possibly County Central Court]
Time:	

If you fail to appear at the time and place above without good cause, you will be deemed to have waived your right to be present at any further proceedings before the Magisterial District Judge, the case will proceed in your absence, and a warrant will be issued for your arrest.

At the preliminary hearing you may:

1. Be represented by counsel;

2. Cross-examine witnesses and inspect physical evidence offered against you;

3. Call witnesses on your behalf other than witnesses to testify to your good reputation only, offer evidence on your behalf and testify;

4. Make written notes of the proceeding, or have your counsel do so, or make a stenographic, mechanical or electronic record of the proceedings.

If you cannot afford to hire an attorney, one may be appointed to represent you. Please contact the office of the Magisterial District Judge for additional information regarding the appointment of an attorney.

If you have any questions, please call the above office immediately.

_____ Date _____

Magisterial District Judge

My commission expires first Monday of January,

If you are disabled and require a reasonable accommodation to gain access to the Magisterial District Court and its services, please contact the Magisterial District Court at the above address or telephone number. We are unable to provide transportation.

COMPLAINT NUMBER:

AOPC 629-06

Appendix 13
Letter Requesting Continuance

[Date]

[District Justice]

Re: Commonwealth of Pennsylvania vs.
       [Defendant]
       Docket No.

Dear [District Justice]:

This office represents [Defendant], currently scheduled for hearing in your office on [Date].   At this time, I am currently attached to the matter of Commonwealth vs. [Defendant 2], [Docket No.] scheduled for Guilty Plea in the [County] Courthouse, at [Time], that same day.

Accordingly, I respectfully request a continuance of [Defendant]'s case to the next available hearing date.

This is the second continuance request in this matter. However, neither the Commonwealth nor the defendant will suffer any prejudice from the granting of this continuance as [Defendant] maintains local residence and is not in danger of fleeing jurisdiction of this Court.

Sincerely,

[Defense Counsel]
cc: Client
       District Attorney

APPENDICES

Appendix 14
Waiver of Preliminary Hearing

COMMONWEALTH OF PENNSYLVANIA
COUNTY OF:

Mag. Dis. No.:

MDJ Honorable Bill Fehringer
124 Pletnick Street
Hometown, PA 19292

Telephone:

**WAIVER OF
PRELIMINARY HEARING**

COMMONWEALTH OF

PENNSYLVANIA

VS.

DEFENDANT: NAME and ADDRESS

Jane Doe
1313 Shiny Mountain Road
Hometown, PA 19292

Docket No.:
Date Filed:

I, the undersigned, certify that I waive my right to a preliminary hearing. I understand that I have a right to this hearing, at which time I have the right to:

1. be represented by counsel,
2. cross-examine witnesses,
3. inspect physical evidence offered against me,
4. call witnesses on my own behalf, offer evidence on my own behalf, and testify,
5. make written notes of the proceedings or have my own counsel do so, and make a stenographic, mechanical, or electronic record of the proceedings.

I understand that if a prima facie case of guilt is not established against me at this hearing, the charges against me would be dismissed.

[ ] I have had a preliminary arraignment during which I was advised of my right to have a preliminary hearing, and of my right to counsel.

[ ] I have received a summons wherein I was advised of my right to have a preliminary hearing and of my right to counsel.

I knowingly, voluntarily, and intelligently make this waiver of my preliminary hearing.

Signed this _____ day of _____, _____

[Defendant's Signature]

(Defendant)

[Defense Counsel Signature]

(Attorney)

Attorney for Defendant (if any)

I HAVE DETERMINED THAT THE DEFENDANT HAS MADE A KNOWING, VOLUNTARY, AND INTELLIGENT WAIVER OF HIS RIGHT TO A PRELIMINARY HEARING.

_____ Date _____ Magisterial District Judge

My commission expires first Monday of January, 2010.

AOPC 601-08

157

Appendix 15
Sample Subpoena Letter

[Date]

[Magisterial District Justice]

Re: *Commonwealth of Pennsylvania vs.*
       [Defendant]
       Docket No.

Dear [Magisterial District Justice]:

This office represents [Defendant] in regard to the above captioned matter and the Preliminary Hearing currently scheduled at your office for the [Date of Hearing]. In order to ensure the relevant facts are elicited at that time I would request subpoenas be issued to the following individual(s):

[Name, last known address, and other contact information of witness]

[Optional] Additionally, I would request that a subpoena duces tecum be issued for said individual to produce the following documents or items of physical evidence:

[Specify which documents or items are to be produced]

Appendix 15
Sample Subpoena Letter

[Optional] As the hearing is currently scheduled for a date within the next 5 days I would also request a continuance of the hearing so as to ensure adequate service of the subpoenas.

The attendance of these individuals [and the production of these documents and items] is essential to the presentation of [Defendant]'s case. I thank you for your time and consideration in this matter.

Sincerely,

[Defense Counsel]

Appendix 16
Petition for Pre-Trial Lineup

[CAPTION]

<u>ORDER</u>

AND NOW, this _____ day of _____, _____, upon consideration of Defendant's Motion for *Pre-Trial Lineup Prior to Preliminary Hearing*. It is hereby ordered that the Commonwealth must present any and all witnesses it intends to call at a preliminary hearing for the above captioned Defendant, to a pre-trial lineup that will be held on the _____ day of _____, _____ at _____ _____m. at the _____ County Prison [or such other location as the Court may direct].

By The Court:

_____

CC: Defense Counsel
       District Attorney
       Magisterial District Judge
       Court Administrator
       Warden, County Prison

Appendix 16
Petition for Pre-Trial Lineup

[CAPTION]
MOTION FOR PRE-TRIAL LINEUP
PRIOR TO PRELIMINARY HEARING

AND NOW, comes the Defendant, by and through her attorneys, and respectfully files this motion for relief, setting forth the following averments:

1. The Defendant was arrested for [charge] on [date].

2. A preliminary hearing is scheduled in front of [District Justice] on [date].

3. [Specify identification in question, for example, "the arresting Officer has alleged that he personally observed the Defendant operating or in actual physical control of the movement of a motor vehicle on the night in question."]

4. Identification of the Defendant is a disputed issue in this matter.

5. The Defendant submits that the officer did not observe the Defendant committing the criminal act.

6. The Defendant's right to dispute the identification will be jeopardized if the witness observes him at the preliminary hearing.

7. The Defendant submits that the witness' memory will be irreparably tainted by observing him at the preliminary hearing.

Appendix 16
Petition for Pre-Trial Lineup

WHEREFORE, the Defendant respectfully requests this Honourable Court order the Commonwealth to produce any witnesses it intends to present at the rescheduled preliminary hearing at a pre-trial lineup, to be held at the County Prison, or other location as the court may direct, in order to protect his rights and prevent any witness' memory from being tainted at the preliminary hearing.

Respectfully submitted,

[Defense Counsel]

Appendix 17
Affidavit of Satisfaction for
Dismissal Pursuant to Rule Crim. Proc. 543(a)

[CAPTION]
AFFIDAVIT OF SATISFACTION

I, [Affiant], Affiant in the above captioned matter do hereby acknowledge that on [date] I did receive payment from [Defendant] in the amount of [amount]. This payment satisfies

[the balance of the returned check and all outstanding fees and costs] or

[the cost of the loss of merchandise and all outstanding fees and costs]

I further submit that there are no outstanding monies due to me by [Defendant] and should this Honourable Court believe a dismissal to be in the public interest, I concur with same.

_____

[Affiant]

Appendix 18
Guilty Plea Colloquy

[CAPTION]

GUILTY PLEA

1.   I am pleading guilty to the following charges:

        Charge   Maximum Penalty

2.   I am aware that the penalties for each of the above charges can be aggregated by the Court at sentencing for a possible total maximum sentence of:

3.   In return for this guilty plea, the Commonwealth has agreed to the following:

4.   I realize that the following mandatory minimum sentences apply:

5.   I realize that there may be increases to my sentence due to the involvement of a weapon, or the nature of the victim, or the location of my crime as follows:

6.   I understand all of the elements of each offense listed above and am guilty of them because, I did the following:

7.   I understand and give up all of the following rights:

-to have a trial by jury or by a judge

-to have the Commonwealth prove my guilt beyond a reasonable doubt

-to participate in the selection of a jury, and to challenge any juror for cause, and/or exercise any preemptory challenges that I would otherwise be entitled to

Appendix 18
Guilty Plea Colloquy

-to cross examine any Commonwealth witness, and to testify or remain silent at trial, or compel any witness on my behalf to testify

-to have an attorney provided to me for free to help at trial if I cannot afford one

-to challenge any illegal evidence

-to give up the presumption of innocence I have, and to give up my right to challenge anything that may have been improper in the investigation and prosecution of my case by the Commonwealth.

8.   I am not mentally disabled or under the influence of any drug or alcohol, nor am I suffering from any disability which affects my own free will, and am free of duress. I am giving up my trial rights knowingly, voluntarily and intelligently.

9.   I retain the right to contest the following on appeal:
    (a)   jurisdiction of the Court
    (b)   legality of the sentence
    (c)   validity of this plea, including claims involving my constitutional right to effective counsel.

10.   I have had an opportunity to discuss this plea agreement with my attorney, with whom I am satisfied. I have read this document in its entirety, understand it completely, and believe this plea is in my best interest.

11.   I understand that the Court is not required to accept this plea agreement, and that if it does not, then I may withdraw this plea.

Appendix 18
Guilty Plea Colloquy

Defendant's Signature _____

Date_____

    I certify with this Defendant that: (1) I have explained this plea agreement and the Defendant's rights; (2) he/she wishes to plead guilty; (3) I have discussed the facts and the law of this case; and (4) I believe the Defendant understands the consequences of pleading guilty.

Attorney for Defendant _____

Date_____

cc: District Attorney
       District Justice

APPENDICES

Appendix 19
Sample OPTM Requesting Remand

[CAPTION]
ORDER OF COURT

AND NOW, this _____ day of _____, upon
consideration of Defendant's Omnibus Pre-Trial Motion, same is
hereby GRANTED, and the above captioned matter is hereby
remanded to the jurisdiction of [Magisterial District Justice] for
a Preliminary Hearing to be scheduled by the District Court.

BY THE COURT,

_____
J.

cc: Defense Counsel
        District Attorney
        Court Administrator

Appendix 19
Sample OPTM Requesting Remand

[CAPTION]
DEFENDANT'S MOTION FOR REMAND

AND NOW, comes the Defendant, by and through her attorneys, and respectfully files the following Omnibus Pre-Trial Motion for Relief.

The Defendant, through his attorney, respectfully avers the following in support of the Motion for Writ of Habeas Corpus:

1.   On [Date of Preliminary Hearing], before [MDJ] a Preliminary Hearing was held in the above captioned matter.

2.   Upon information available at that time the Defendant agreed to waive her right to cross-examine witnesses and inspect the evidence against her based upon the District Attorney's representation that she was ARD eligible.

3.   On [Date subsequent] the District Attorney's Office informed Counsel for the Defendant that she is not ARD eligible at this time.

4.   Accordingly, the Defendant wishes to fight the charges against her, in that she avers she has a meritorious defense to same, and that the charges are not supported by the evidence.

5.   Defendant further submits that the Commonwealth is unable to establish a *Prima Facie* case against Defendant.

Appendix 19
Sample OPTM Requesting Remand

WHEREFORE, the Petitioner requests this Honourable Court to hold a hearing inquiring into the facts of the case to determine whether *Prima Facie* evidence exists, or in the alternative, to remand the case for a remedial preliminary hearing at the Office of the District Justice.

Respectfully submitted,

[Defense Counsel]

Appendix 20
Motion to Correct Transcript

[CAPTION]
<u>ORDER OF COURT</u>

AND NOW, this _____, day of _____, _____, based upon the Defendant's Motion to Correct Transcript, same is hereby GRANTED, and the Transcript of Record from the Preliminary Hearing held on the [Date] before [MDJ] is corrected as follows:

[Specify correction]

BY THE COURT

_____

Defense Counsel
District Attorney
Court Administrator
Magisterial District Justice

APPENDICES

Appendix 20
Motion to Correct Transcript

[CAPTION]

MOTION TO CORRECT TRANSCRIPT

AND NOW, comes the Defendant, by and through his attorneys, and respectfully avers the following:

1. The Defendant was scheduled to have a preliminary hearing on [Date], at [Magisterial District Justice].
2. The Defendant and the arresting officer agreed that the charge of Reckless Driving would be withdrawn in exchange for the Defendant waiving all other charges.
3. Prior to arraignment Defendant was notified that he could not be considered for the ARD program as a result of his waiving the Reckless Driving charge.
4. Defendant submits that he did not waive the Reckless Driving Charge.
5. Defendant submits that had it not been for the withdrawal of the Reckless Driving charge, he would not have waived the other charges at his preliminary hearing.
6. Defense counsel spoke with [District Attorney] on [Date], regarding this matter, and was told that he would look into this issue.
7. To date, there has been no communication from the District Attorney's office regarding this matter.

WHEREFORE, the Defendant respectfully requests your Honourable Court to schedule a hearing to correct the defects on the transcript issued from [Magisterial District Justice].

Respectfully submitted,

[Defense Counsel]

Appendix 21
Motion for Bail Reduction

[CAPTION]
O R D E R

AND   NOW,   this   _____   day   of
_____, _____, upon consideration of
the attached Motion for Bail Reduction, same is hereby
GRANTED, and the conditions of Defendant's Bail Bond are
modified as follows:

[Specify whether your client is seeking a reduction in the
bail amount, the return of documents, the right to visit a place,
the right to communicate with other parties, etc.]

BY THE COURT:

_____
J.

cc: Defense Counsel
       District Attorney
       Court Administrtor
       Bail Surety

Appendix 21
Motion for Bail Reduction

[CAPTION]
PETITION FOR REDUCTION OF BAIL

AND NOW, comes the Defendant, by and through his attorney, and petitions this Honourable Court to reduce the bail set in the above captioned matter, upon the following:

1. That [Defendant] was arrested on [Date] for a warrant charging [specify charges].
2. That the charge(s) in question arise(s) from alleged incidents which occurred more than five years ago.
3. That [Defendant] is currently being detained in the _____ County Correctional Facility in lieu of one million dollars ($1,000,000.00) bail.
4. That [Defendant] does not have the financial wherewithal or ability to post the said bail.
5. That [Defendant] is [age] and is currently employed by [employer].
6. That [Defendant] currently resides at [address], Pennsylvania with [spouse, children, or other parties] that he [owns or rents] has resided in [County]for a period of [specify time].
7. That [Defendant] has no prior criminal record.
8. That [Defendant] is a member in good standing of the [specify church or civic organization] and has been so for [specify time].
9. That [Defendant] has significant familial and economic ties to the community.

Appendix 21
Motion for Bail Reduction

10.   That [Defendant] is not a risk of flight, and is not charged with using any false identification or alias.

11.   That [Defendant] will appear at all times required of him if released on bail.

WHEREFORE, your Movant respectfully requests this Honourable Court to reduce the said bail in the above captioned matter and that he be released on his own recognizance.

Respectfully submitted,

[Defense Counsel]

APPENDICES

Appendix 22
Motion to Quash Refiling

[CAPTION]

O R D E R

AND NOW, this _____ day of
_____, _____, upon consideration of
Defendant's Motion to Quash the Refiling of Charges, it is
hereby ORDERED that Defendant's motion is GRANTED, and
the Commonwealth is forever precluded from refiling the
following charges in relation to the incident(s) arising out of the
following charges:

[Specify charges here]

BY THE COURT:

_____
J.

cc: Defense Counsel
District Attorney
District Justice
Court Administrator

Appendix 22
Motion to Quash Refiling

[CAPTION]

MOTION TO QUASH REFILING OF CHARGES

AND NOW, comes [Defendant] by his attorneys, and respectfully avers the following:

1. [Defendant] is currently charged with [specify charges]
2. [Defendant] is scheduled for a Preliminary Hearing before [District Justice] on [specify date]
3. [Defendant] was previously charged with similar offenses before [District Justice], and after a preliminary hearing and a full and fair opportunity for the Commonwealth to present its evidence, same was dismissed.
4. [Specify]
    a. The Commonwealth has now refilled these charges as part of an ongoing pattern of harassment and offensive tactics, designed to overcome the will of [Defendant].
    b. As the incident in question is alleged to have occurred on [specify date] the refilled charges are beyond the applicable statute of limitations. [specify statute subsection].
5. Accordingly, the refilled charges should be quashed.
6. Additionally, to prevent subjecting the Defendant from continued harassment, the Commonwealth should be forever precluded from filing charges arising out of the incident in question

Appendix 22
Motion to Quash Refiling

WHEREFORE, the defendant respectfully requests this Honourable Court to forever preclude the Commonwealth from refiling the instant charges against [Defendant].

Respectfully submitted,

[Defense Counsel]

Appendix 23
Sample Motion for Writ of Habeas Corpus

[CAPTION]
<u>ORDER OF COURT</u>

AND NOW, this _____ day of _____ _____, upon consideration of Defendant's Pre-Trial Motion, a hearing in the above captioned matter shall be held on the _____ day of _____, at _____ o'clock ____.m. in Court Room No. _____, _____ County Courthouse, _____, Pennsylvania, at which time the Court will allow Defendant's Counsel to inquire into the facts supporting the charges filed against him/her.

BY THE COURT,

_____
J.

cc: Defense Counsel
        District Attorney
        Court Administrator

178

Appendix 23
Sample Motion for Writ of Habeas Corpus

[CAPTION]
<u>DEFENDANT'S MOTION FOR WRIT OF HABEAS CORPUS</u>

1. On [Date of Preliminary Hearing], the Preliminary Hearing was held.
2. Defendant submits that during the Preliminary Hearing, the Commonwealth failed to establish a *Prima Facie* case against Defendant.
3. Defendant submits that no testimony establishing the Defendant's presence at the scene or connection with the criminal offense was introduced.
4. Defendant submits that the testimony which was presented is not competent evidence which could be introduced at trial for a jury's consideration.
5. Defendant further submits that the testimony which was presented failed to establish a prima facie case as to [cite specific element of the offense charged].

WHEREFORE, the Petitioner requests this Honourable Court to schedule a hearing on the above captioned matter at which time the Commonwealth should be required to submit competent evidence capable of establishing a prima facie case or else be faced with a dismissal of [charge] against Defendant.

Respectfully submitted,

[Defense Counsel]

Appendix 24
Pre-Trial Motion to Hold a Competency Hearing

[CAPTION]
ORDER OF COURT

AND NOW, this [Date], upon consideration of the Defendant's Motion to hold a Competency Hearing, a hearing is scheduled for the _____ day of _____, _____ in Courtroom No. ____ of the _____ County Courthouse. At that time the Defendant will be permitted to examine the testimony of [witness] in regards to his/her competency to testify.

Furthermore, [witness] is to be examined by [Local Mental Health Professional such as a psychiatrist] for a mental health evaluation, the contents of which will be disclosed only to this Court and Counsel for the Commonwealth and Defendant. Same to be completed within the next 15 days.

The Commonwealth is hereby Ordered to secure the appearance of [witness] at the mental health evaluation and at the time of the hearing.

BY THE COURT,

_____

cc: [District Attorney]
       [Defense Counsel]
       [Mental Heatlh Professional]

Appendix 24
Pre-Trial Motion to Hold a Competency Hearing

[CAPTION]

MOTION FOR COMPETENCY HEARING

The Defendant, through his attorney, respectfully avers the following in support of this Motion to hold a competency evaluation:

1. Taint is the implantation of false memories or distortion of actual memories through improper and suggestive interview techniques.

2. The Pennsylvania Supreme Court has held that taint is a legitimate question for examination at a competency hearing in cases involving complaints of sexual abuse made by minors.

3. The Commonwealth has submitted that the alleged sexual abuse occurred while the alleged victim was a minor.

4. There has been a period of 2 (two) years between the first such alleged encounter and the reporting of the alleged abuse.

5. The Commonwealth has admitted that the alleged victim spoke with several individuals, including friends, family members, school guidance counselors, victim counselors, and psychologists or psychiatrists.

6. The Defendant submits that the Commonwealth's only witness to the alleged events may have been tainted by her conversations with these people

7. The Defendant submits that evidence of possible taint already exists with regard to the alleged victims actions in that she first reported the

Appendix 24
Pre-Trial Motion to Hold a Competency Hearing

> alleged incidents as dreams, and only later after much prodding did she allege sexual abuse.

8. The victim of a crime of sexual violence may be compelled to undergo a psychiatric examination where there are compelling reasons or a showing of a particularized necessity for such an examination.

WHEREFORE, the Defendant respectfully requests this Honourable Court to require [witness] to undergo a Mental Health Evaluation to determine if she suffers from a mental illness and/or can differentiate realtiy from dreams, and also to hold a competency hearing, at which point Defense Counsel may inquire as to the nature of her ability to accurately recall the incidents in question.

Appendix 25
Petition for Allowance to Withdraw

[CAPTION]

<u>O R D E R</u>

AND NOW, this _____ day of
_____, _____, upon consideration of
[Defense Counsel]'s Petition to Withdraw, same is hereby
GRANTED and [Defense Counsel] is relieved of further
representation of Defendant in this matter.

Defendant is directed to retain new counsel, seek an
application for representation by the Public Defender's Office,
or file a Petition to Proceed Pro Se, within 10 days of the entry
of this Order.

BY THE COURT:

_____
J.

cc: [Defense Counsel]
        District Attorney
        Defendant
        Clerk of Courts

Appendix 25
Petition for Allowance to Withdraw

[CAPTION]
<u>PETITION FOR ALLOWANCE TO WITHDRAW</u>

AND NOW, comes [Defense Counsel], attorney of record for the Defendant in the above captioned matters, and submits this Petition for Allowance to Withdraw upon the following representations, to wit:

1. That your Petitioner is counsel of record for the Defendant in the above captioned cases.

2. That your Petitioner began representation of the Defendant with the understanding that Defendant would reimburse your Petitioner for fees and costs incurred in the course of representation.

3. That to date the Defendant has failed to remit payment for legal fees, costs for Court Reporter, and the production of documents.

4. That your petitioner is unable to effectively represent the Defendant to the best of his abilities and in harmony with the Pennsylvania Rules of Professional Conduct in the absence of such payment.

5. That the Defendant had a Preliminary Hearing before [MDJ] on [Date], at which time all charges were bound over for trial.

6. That the Defendant is currently scheduled for arraignment on [Date].

7. That Defendant has sufficient time to secure alternate counsel by this date, and will not be prejudiced by Defense Counsel's recusal.

APPENDICES

Appendix 25
Petition for Allowance to Withdraw

WHEREFORE, your Petitioner respectfully requests this Honourable Court to allow him to withdraw his appearance in the above captioned matters.

Respectfully submitted

[Defense Counsel]

Appendix 26
Request for Interpreter

[DATE]

[RECIPIENT]

Re: *Commonwealth of Pennsylvania vs.*
        Defendant
        Docket No.

Dear [Magisterial District Justice]:

This office represents [Defendant] in the above captioned matter, currently scheduled for a Preliminary Hearing before your Honour on [Date and Time]. As your Honour may be aware, [Defendant] is a naturalized citizen of the United States, originally from [Country]. Her native tongue is [specify language], and she only speaks limited English as a second language.

After further consult with my client, it is clear that she does not speak or comprehend the English language to a degree sufficient to enable her to participate in her own defense at the time of the Preliminary Hearing. Accordingly, I would request the appearance of a Court approved interpreter for translation of testimony from English to [specify language]. Additionally, should my client choose to testify at the time of the Hearing, the interpreter would be required to translate my client's testimony from [specify language] to English.

186

Appendix 26
Request for Interpreter

Should your Honour require any further documentation or information, please feel free to contact me at this office.

Sincerely,

[Defense Counsel]

cc: Client
       District Attorney

Appendix 27
Follow up Letter to District Attorney

[Date]

[District Attorney]

Re: *Commonwealth of Pennsylvania vs.*
       Defendant
       Docket No.

Dear [District Attorney]:

This letter is just in follow up to our appearance on [Date], before [Magisterial District Justice] with regard to the above captioned criminal matter. At that time, we agreed to waive into Court [specify charge(s)], a [felony/misdemeanor] with the expectation that [Defendant] will be entering a plea at some time in the future. In consideration of that waiver, your office agreed to [consider for ARD, withdraw some other charge, reduce the set bail, etc].

I appreciate your professionalism and courtesy in this regard and I know that [Defendant] does as well. In the meantime, should any other concerns arise, feel free to contact me.

Sincerely,

[Defense Counsel]

Appendix 28
Follow up Letter to Client

[Date]

[Defendant]

Re: *Commonwealth of Pennsylvania vs.*
      Defendant
      Docket No.

Dear [Defendant]:

This letter is just in follow up to your hearing before [MDJ] on [Date]. At that time we appeared and cross-examined the police officer involved in this matter with an eye toward filing possible suppression issues at a later date. A court reporter was present, and a transcript will be produced and forwarded to your attention as soon as it is available.

Despite our legal arguments and cross-examination, the District Justice held that there was sufficient evidence to bind the charges over for trial. Additionally, your bail was continued and you were instructed to contact [Police Department] in order to arrange for fingerprinting and photographing. Your next appearance will be at arraignment at the Court of Common Pleas on [Date, if known]. You will receive further correspondence from this office indicating the time of that appearance and whether or not we can waive your appearance.

This office's fee to represent you through arraignment and pre-trial motions is [amount if flat fee, otherwise specify retainer request], due 30 days before the time of arraignment. Should the case proceed to trial, an additional [amount] will be due 30 days before the call of the criminal list. Please contact this office's billing manager if you have any questions in this regard.

Appendix 28
Follow up Letter to Client

Should you have any questions or concerns related to your case, feel free to contact me.

Sincerely,

[Defense Counsel]

APPENDICES

Appendix 29
Follow up Letter to Client (ARD Eligible)

[Date]

[Defendant]

Re: *Commonwealth of Pennsylvania vs.*
Defendant
Docket No.

Dear [Defendant]:

This letter is just in follow up to your preliminary hearing before [Magisterial District Justice] on [Date]. At that time we appeared and pursuant to the representation of the District Attorney that you are eligible for the ARD program agreed to waive the charges against you into Court. As previously discussed, this Program does not result in a criminal conviction. Rather, you are on probation for a period of time to be set by the Court and so long as you successfully complete that Program, the charges are dismissed. However, the ARD is recorded on your Pennsylvania driving record, so that a second arrest would result in a second offense DUI with a mandatory minimum term of incarceration.

In terms of procedure, you need to complete the following:

[specify the local requirements of the program, including whether or not the client has to schedule a CRN or Drug and Alcohol analysis within the immediate future. Many counties also require a background check and initial probation appointment, as well as up-front fees which may be as much as $500 or more for processing. Also provide your client with telephone numbers for the relevant agencies so that he or she can easily contact them.]

Appendix 29
Follow up Letter to Client (ARD Eligible)

In terms of future court appearances, I would expect to have the ARD scheduled within [specify time period depending on locality], once all of your paperwork has been processed. You should anticipate being eligible for actual entry into the Program in approximately [specify time]. On the ARD court hearing date, you need to have someone drive you to court. You will be physically handing in your driver's license at that court proceeding.

Your license will be suspended for a period of [30 or 60] days.

At the end of that period, you need to have your license restored through PennDOT. If you are caught driving during that period, the District Attorney's Office will petition to have your ARD status revoked. Additionally, you will face a summary charge, which carries a mandatory minimum period of incarceration and a significant fine. As I mentioned in our earlier meetings, you will be on probation for [time period] and you will also have to complete all drug and alcohol classes as ordered by the Court.

In order for this office to continue to represent you through the ARD process an additional fee in the amount of [specify amount if flat fee, or indicate if taken on retainer] is due 30 days before your scheduled appearance in Court. Should you be ineligible for the ARD program, or if the case should proceed to trial then other fees may apply, please contact this office's billing manager for details.

Feel free to contact me at this office with any questions or concerns you have related to your case.

Sincerely,

[Defense Counsel]

www.ingramcontent.com/pod-product-compliance
Lightning Source LLC
Chambersburg PA
CBHW021426180326
41458CB00001B/148

9 780578 000343